DISCERNING THE **GOLD** IN HUMAN EXPERIENCE

Leadership Faith and Organizations

Christine Anderson fcJ

authorHOUSE

AuthorHouse™ UK
1663 Liberty Drive
Bloomington, IN 47403 USA
www.authorhouse.co.uk
Phone: UK TFN: 0800 0148641 (Toll Free inside the UK)
       UK Local: 02036 956322 (+44 20 3695 6322 from outside the UK)

© 2021 Christine Anderson fcJ. All rights reserved.

No part of this book may be reproduced, stored in a retrieval system, or transmitted by any means without the written permission of the author.

Published by AuthorHouse 05/06/2021

ISBN: 978-1-6655-8498-2 (sc)
ISBN: 978-1-6655-8500-2 (hc)
ISBN: 978-1-6655-8499-9 (e)

Print information available on the last page.

This book is printed on acid-free paper.

Because of the dynamic nature of the Internet, any web addresses or links contained in this book may have changed since publication and may no longer be valid. The views expressed in this work are solely those of the author and do not necessarily reflect the views of the publisher, and the publisher hereby disclaims any responsibility for them.

Contents

Acknowledgements vii
Dedication ix
Foreword by John Bazalgette.. xi
Preface... xvii

Chapter 1   The Gold of Experience 1
Chapter 2   The Gold of the History and Mystery of Life 9
Chapter 3   The Gold of Creative Emerging Newness 19
Chapter 4   Gold Melted and Transformed 31
Chapter 5   Gold Tried in the Furnace of Life 39
Chapter 6   The Gold of Transforming Roles...............................49
Chapter 7   The Gold of Crisis and Faith 65
Chapter 8   The Gold of Clarity and Confusion 71
Chapter 9   The Gold of Wisdom in Experience..........................83
Chapter 10 The Gold of Collective Wisdom 89

Acknowledgements

Scripture quotations from the Jerusalem Bible.
All photographs included with permission.
Cover design by Marie Claire Sykes, FCJ.

Dedication

To the colleagues, participants, and friends who have accompanied this journey.

To the Sisters Faithful Companions of Jesus, especially Katherine Mary O'Flynn and Marie Claire Sykes. In their role of international leaders of the congregation they supported this international work, and to all those members who quietly encouraged and challenged me on the way.

To the executive boards of UISG (International Union of Superior Generals) and to the executive secretary Patricia Murray, ibvm, who encouraged many leadership teams to avail of the training on offer through Faith and Praxis for Global Leadership.

To the international teams of Young Christian Workers resident in Rome.

To the current and past staff, associates and board members of the Craighead Institute including the current director Dr. Lisa Curtis, Anne Macdonald, Alan McKell, Dr. Noel Donnelly, Professor Bart McGettrick, Jim Christie SJ, Professor Duncan McLaren, Rev. John Harvey, Maureen McGuigan, Esther Brannan, Eileen Hill and so many others.

To the staff of Faith and Praxis for Global Leadership: my successor and current director, Emili Turu Rofes, FMS; the coordinator of the Africa programs Maria Pilar Benavente Serrano, Msola, Monika Kopacz; Frances Heery; Marian Murcia HFB; and Maria Tanti Galea.

To the African associates: Micheline Kenda HFB, Congolese board member in Rome; Caroline Njah, program coordinator in Cameroon, Immaculate Nakato SMR program leader and facilitator, Eastern Africa; Jules Adanbéché Hounkponou, from Benin and program leader West Africa; Dominic Apee Ayine MAf, associate in Ghana; Wenceslaus Kwindingwi CMM from Zimbabwe and associate program leader in Tanzania. Also to Gertrud Glotzbach Msola for her unfailing administrative assistance.

To the consultants of the Grubb Institute of Behavioural Studies John Bazalette, Jean Hutton Reed, and Colin Quine, for their endless patience and sharing of knowledge in both the Craighead Institute and Faith and Praxis for Global Leadership.

Finally, a heartfelt thank-you to my family, friends, and participants and the many benefactors without whom these institutes in Glasgow and Rome, as also the projects in Africa, would never have developed and thrived.

Foreword by John Bazalgette

Discerning the Gold in Human Experience

When President Barack Obama went to Africa for the first time in July 2009, he said, 'Africa does not need strong men. It needs strong institutions.'[1] He was speaking to the Parliament in Accra, the capital of Ghana, and he challenged Africans and Westerners alike: Africa needs partnerships, not patronage.[2] This view puts into real and significant perspective Christine Anderson FCJ's fascinating account of her life's work as a member of the Society of the Sisters Faithful Companions of Jesus. This is a book by a 'strong woman', much of whose work has been in Africa and which has always been directed towards building strong and resilient institutions based on collaboration and co-creation.

Early in the book, the author describes an experience in Central Africa when facilitating an assembly of missionaries.

---

[1] See Hilary Clinton's account of being Obama's Secretary of State in the book *Hard Choices* (Simon and Schuster, 2014), 270.

[2] There also a little unintended 'coincidence' between Obama's view and that fact that the author has titled her book *Discerning the Gold in Human Experience*: before independence in 1957 Ghana was called the Gold Coast!

The area was poor and war-torn with another war just about to break out. In the evening, I walked on the dry, cracked earth where absolutely nothing was growing so food was short. On my walk, I met an elderly woman who was not part of my group. I remarked to her about the drought and how difficult life was in that area. She looked me straight in the eye and said, 'Yes but it is not just the land that is dry; our hearts are dry!' I was so moved by her evident pain but also her hope as we continued to converse and heard her say she did not need the West only to be bringing material gifts, useful as they are, but she needed us to help her discover meaning and light within this dire situation. With her, I recognized her thirst for meaning, and it inflamed my desire to work at meaning with groups of people in equally dried-out situations at home and abroad.[3]

The author describes her response, which was not to turn to that elderly African person, seeing her as a case to be evangelized—as could have been the temptation, given that she was facilitating forty missionaries at the time. She tells the reader that that remark inflamed her desire to explore truly refreshing meaning in groups and institutions. The challenge for her and for any Christian working with lived experience and having a faith that God is real is to ask oneself, 'What is God already doing here, and how does our faith permeate what is happening here?'

---

[3] See her script Chapter Two.

At the core of her work is her passion about integrating life and faith. It is important to note the order in which she puts those two: *life* and *faith*. For her, faith provides a lens to use to explore and reveal the meaning of lived lives. This understanding of faith is not something which imposes its shape on reality. It is not about dogma but about the ability to live with uncertainty. As a member of a congregation inspired by the spirituality of Saint Ignatius, this is no surprise. Drawing on the heart of this spirituality, she steps confidently into working with 'the confusion, the busyness, the worries, and perplexities that are the very stuff of our experience' of life in organizations, especially as these challenge their leaders. In fact, every institution continually exists on the edge of chaos—and the temptation for inept leaders is to conceal that fact by seeking to convince others that they are the ones who can deliver what is yearned for. For the author, leadership is about truth, not about imposing imaginary solutions but taking the first step to propose ways of understanding the reality of the forces and factors at work in the organization's real life and, as that shared understanding takes shape, to elaborate purposeful ways for engaging with reality. The dialectic and methodology of Cardinal Joseph Cardijn, the founder of the Young Christian Workers offers a methodology of see-judge-act that is indelibly written into her way of working. Given the frequency with which she has worked in war-torn places and other high-risk areas, Pope Francis would probably say that she also shares with him the aphorism from the German poet-philosopher Friedrich Hölderlin: 'Where the danger is, also grows the saving power.'[4]

---

[4] Pope Francis and Austen Ivereigh, *Let Us Dream: The Path to a Better Future* (London: Simon and Schuster, 2020), 6.

Every project to which she has committed herself and those who work with her is not a job but a way of life. Together with competent teams, she is not passing on academic theories of leadership to be debated in symposia. She works practically, with robust concepts that are interpreted and made effective in her own way. These include leadership for an unknown future; systemic leadership, seen as a leadership that makes connections; leadership of disruption and discontinuity; prophetic leadership; leadership of flexibility and spirals; leadership that 'does theology' in a time of unknowing; faith-filled leadership; and of key importance, accountability. She describes the methodologies she has used which show how practitioners can use these tools to integrate life and faith effectively in a diversity of cultures other than her own Scottish origins. Some of these concepts and methods were developed in collaboration with the Grubb Institute, but in her hands, they have become her own.

Some of today's most important professional thinking and methodology focuses seriously on the significance of relating leadership in the secular world to the growing understanding of the cosmos.[5] And here lies the promise of a challenging path forward in future thinking and training in leadership for Christians concerned with our present ways of life. In this, the author follows the leadership offered by Pope Francis in the book *Let Us Dream*. Just as he argues from his experience as a member of the Society of Jesus, this author feels that what she has learned is of general relevance to society as a whole. Religious congregations have much to gain and to contribute by sharing their experience in a wide context.

---

[5] See for example Gordon Lawrence, *Tongued with Fire: Groups in Experience*, published in 2000 by Karnac Books, especially the chapters 'The Management of Oneself in Role' and 'Signals of Transcendence'.

There is a golden thread that runs in and out through the whole of Christine Anderson's account of her life and work. This is the centrality of working in role. In this book, she shows how she has lived and goes on living in role as a member of her own community of the Faithful Companions of Jesus. As a result, she offers us one example and sets a standard of working with people, whose hearts are dry from the way too many institutions are led and managed. She invites us to see, judge, and act in any of our own roles in life. In this wholly appropriate way, she shows us that as a woman, working always with teams of professional colleagues, she has been building strong institutions in Glasgow and Rome. The leaders of those strong institutions have learnt that they have no need to compete with one another: in fact, the call to them is to collaborate, to partner one another and work together—whether they know it or not—in building the kingdom of God for which Christians pray whenever we say the Lord's Prayer.

It would be a mistake to read this book as if it were solely addressed to Christians or even only to people with a 'religious' faith. That is why this foreword deliberately opens with a quotation from an American president, the leader of the most powerful nation in the world at the time.

As that quotation implies, this book has two central messages for all those in leadership positions.

Every leader who intends to lead an effective organization will do so by attending to their experience, not as a 'person-based' experience but as an institutional experience, which is telling them about the forces and factors at work in their institution's dynamic interactions with its context. *Those institution/context interactions frame everything that happens*—seldom in expected ways! Effective leaders know that they are human sensors whose primary task is to learn to make sense of what their experience is telling them about those interactions. From that, they can discern both the path opening up in front of them and the spirit which energizes their institution, carrying it forward institutionally. In this book, the author explores how she has learnt to lead authentically and how she has taught others to do the same.

The second message invites any reader to step back far enough from the text on the page and to notice that this book is written by a strong woman. As we look around the world today, we notice how many strong women are working in leadership positions. Note also that Pope Francis underlines the importance of women being given leadership in his own institution. He has a determined policy to make their wisdom felt in its highest positions. The scriptural approach to wisdom is to understand it as a feminine quality, nestling in the beating heart of institutional strength. He is telling us that strong institutions in today's world need to gain their strength from wisdom in their leaders.

The idea of seeing one's experience as a treasured resource offers a holistic approach to developing wisdom in the formation of leaders by paying attention to the wise leadership listed at the heart of the book and in the critical paradigm shift described in chapter 10. I am sure that Barack Obama would agree with the author!

John Bazalgette
Organizational consultant and writer
Founding member of the Grubb Institute
London, 2021

Preface

This book takes the form of a series of experiences and experiential methodologies. It is written as one experience among many for those seeking to work effectively with small and large faith-based groups in NGOs, voluntary organizations, and international organizations. These particular groups desire, in different ways, to contribute to building a more just world and to integrating their values, beliefs, and faith with their life experience. I have journeyed with many African, Asia, Oceanian, and European colleagues and participants for the last thirty years. My focus now is to share the methodologies and processes with these peoples who have enriched my learning, my thinking, and my faith. I hope that, in doing so, the readers will be inspired to reflect on their own experiences and discover the treasures within themselves.

My passion has always been to find a way to integrate life experience and faith, values, and beliefs—seeing them as one human story and avoiding the fragmentation wrought upon us today by so many complex systems. Throughout all this work, the desire was to work professionally, deeply, and effectively with people who come from different faith backgrounds with different values and beliefs in areas struggling for development and wholeness.

Some locations and names of individuals have been changed, and there is no intent to identify the origins of some of the examples. The processes described owe much to the International Christian Worker Movements, to the Craighead Institute for the Integration of Life and Faith in Scotland that I directed for sixteen years, and to the Grubb Institute of Behavioural Studies London, where I trained as an organizational role analyst. The processes were then used extensively in Faith and Praxis for Global Leadership in Rome and many countries of the world, particularly in Africa. All of the writing is influenced by my own life as a member of the Society of Sisters Faithful Companions of Jesus who live out of the basic spirituality of St Ignatius of Loyola.

Most of these experiences were gained in a variety of organizations—family groups, workers' organizations, neighbourhoods, refugees camps, local justice and peace groups, and ecclesial and international organizations. It was in the latter part of my life, in Faith and Praxis in Rome, that I worked more with members of International Congregations of women and men religious. The methodologies were similar in both cases and the experiences, though vastly different in their expression of the organizations, were alike in always working from experience. The processes were robust enough to be the containers for new learning and development.

Throughout my life, we worked in teams, and I owe much to the dedicated members who joined me. Maureen McGuigan, SND, developed the Integrating Life and Faith Program with me in Glasgow, and Maria Pilar Benavente Serrano Msola spearheaded the leadership programs in Africa with Immaculate Nakato, SMR, responsible for the programs in Eastern Africa and Mr Jules Adanchédé Hounkponou in Benin and Western Africa.

L-R Dr Lisa Curtis Director of Craighead Institute with Ms. Anne Macdonald

I have been encouraged to write this book by many colleagues, donors and participants. The background to some of the activity is described through the filter of my own experience. The reason for this is that the programs we developed are experiential and so emerge wherever they are delivered today out of the experience of the teams and participants in their particular contexts and cultures. By experiential, I mean that they were designed to engage both the mind and the heart, both theory and application, and always start from the experience of the participants. This means that the staff also engage with their own experience and find ways to reflect on it. My hope is that this book will contribute to the ongoing reflection and action in today's world and that those who read it will find some light for their own journey, which will be theirs, not mine.

As a Christian, I am fascinated by the gap that can exist between what we say we believe and how we apply that in daily life. It has been my life's work to explore the meaning of experience in life, to search new questions, to open up closed subjects, and to allow freedom of expression in a culture that at times can try to shut this sort of attitude down. In this book, I have reflected with the readers on part of my own story, a life lived in a religious congregation. I discovered early on that experiences need strong processes not just for personal reflection but for transformation in society. The basis of our work was always the context, especially civic society. My heart was always with those Christians who were engaged in social justice and were trying to bring about social change.

Chapter One tells the story of my experience, an experience that inspired both the Craighead Institute of Life and Faith in Glasgow and Faith and Praxis for Global Leadership in Rome.

Chapters 2 to 4 describe some of the content and processes used whilst working with groups.

Chapter 5 focuses on Praxis events and Organizational Role Analysis.

Chapter 6 looks at faith-filled organizational development.

Chapter 7 explores diversity and crisis in organizations.

Chapter 8 highlights the gift of vulnerability in organizations.

Chapter 9 refers to growth and diminishment in international organizations.

Chapter 10 reflects on the tension between faith and experience and how it is an ongoing story.

CHAPTER 1

The Gold of Experience

My own journey started in a Christian Worker Movement in Britain—at that time known as Family and Social Action and later transformed into the World of Work. It was there that first I learned that experience is our greatest resource—not simply the experience of the past but experience analysed and reflected on so that it moved me to a new place for transformation and for the future. I learned this from Patrick Keegan former international president of the Young Christian Workers, who encouraged me to treasure every experience, to write about it, and to note my insights in a logbook. This discipline transformed my being and my thinking. I am so grateful for the analytic approach, even if, at times, it led to misunderstandings with others who preferred a systematic approach. I joined the International Society of the Sisters' Faithful Companions of Jesus in the 1960s, expecting to spend my life in a convent. The training there was very strict. The community, we were told, was contemplative in action, and we learned to live from within. It was in my early years both in my family and in the community that I learned to live with an internal spirit of faith in God, different from a set of beliefs and rituals or preconceived ideas. Later, from Patrick Keegan, I learned to question everything and explore meaning in the crevices of the experiences that we so easily glide over. It is a gift that has never left me and something I have sought to share as widely as possible in my own engagement with society and in different contexts.

L-R Marie Geneviève Renaud, Veronika Schreiner and Christine Anderson FCJ Kairos Community

In the Christian Worker Movement, I rediscovered a passion not just for faith but also for the integration of faith and experience. This led to the foundation of an institute of training, research, and consultancy in Glasgow City Centre, Scotland, known as the Craighead Institute for the Integration of Life and Faith. It was the beginning of my journeys to many countries with teams of colleagues to share this vision on request. It was an extraordinary journey leading me during the next thirty years to engage in training and consultancy events in many countries in four continents. The same theme was always at the heart of it: how can our experience of life and of faith transform our organizations in pastoral, educational, and social settings through skilled leaders and engaged staff and members? Activities and events are not the substance of the work of the Institute but the *vehicles of change,* and it is timely to question the *transformative nature* of our work. The mission of the institute is to work at the integration of life and faith not for itself alone but with a view to effecting change in society that touches the lives of those most on the margins or who are directly affected by unjust structures.

A year after I had started the Craighead Institute in Glasgow, I reconnected with some colleagues of the Grubb Institute of Behavioural Studies, whom I first met when they were conducting an educational project in the Archdiocese of Westminster. I collaborated with them in a small way, and later, my community leader encouraged me to pursue a professional development in organizational role analysis in the Grubb Institute. Demanding as it was, it was also exhilarating, and it fed into my desire to work at the transformation of organizations, not only faith-based ones but all those grappling with injustice and oppression in the poorer echelons of society in Europe and particularly in Africa and Asia. During this time, my community base was in Scotland with two other members who were giving retreats and accompanying people according to the spirituality of St Ignatius of Loyola. This kept me rooted in the spirituality of the community in which we had all been formed and which sustained not just our prayer and our faith but the very meaning of our lives.

It was hard both for my companions and for me that I was coming and going all the time, and what I learned in that time was that experience is not easily transferable! However a disconnect can occur when we do not share the same experience. We tried successfully and unsuccessfully at times to live with difference, and although we did not grow away from each other, we did live different lifestyles within the same corporate mission. This was new in the community I joined because in the early days, every member taught in a school or was associated with a school or college and returned home to the same convent every night. In these circumstances, we were living with different works but shared the same mission, which was to be companions of Jesus and companions to each other. Now in the twenty-first century, this disconnect is not as exceptional as many members of the community work individually in different organizations. Because of the changing context and needs of society, our international community has taken on a different face whilst living the same mission.

After sixteen years in the Glasgow institute, I was asked to go to Rome and work as human resources officer for Jesuit Refugee Service (JRS) International. It was a natural evolution for me as the institute was well established and for me meant the development of work in Africa and Asia. I had so many opportunities and experiences and at that time felt overwhelmed by the misery I met as well the capacity for resilience and joy of the refugees. However, the learning achieved in the worker movements and in Craighead Institute stood me in good stead, and the next phase of my life was applying that in a wider context. I want to share some of the theories developed during those years with you, the readers, but the learning will be yours as you apply an experiential approach working with many dynamics enabling the integration of faith and life in your own cultures and contexts. My spirituality is that of St Ignatius of Loyola. However, the methodology and processes can be easily developed in your local cultures and ways of living your own spirituality.

In Rome, my congregation developed Faith and Praxis for Global Leadership as a legal entity to facilitate this training both in leadership and membership in organizations and to train facilitators and consultants for the future. A basic principle was that as far as possible, we worked as teams of associates,

Discerning the Gold in Human Experience

acknowledging that the lone charismatic person was in danger of building their own realm and using it as a power base. In Rome, we worked with the international leadership of communities, numbering from one hundred to several thousand members, and were privileged to accompany these leadership teams for part of their journey. Five of the leaders, who were participants in the Rome program, requested that we go to Africa and share our processes and methodologies with leadership teams there, and it was firstly in Uganda that we developed the Training the Trainers program with our African colleagues. Today, the African colleagues use this training to run similar programs for their own people.

I first worked in Africa with Jesuit Refugee Service (JRS) in Zimbabwe, Rwanda, Burundi, Congo, Ivory Coast, Liberia, and Kenya. My contribution to the lives of the refugees was a drop in a vast ocean of suffering and deprivation in the camps and in the projects. At that time, I worked with the local team members and staff groups as human resources officer and ended with an organizational review of the organization as commissioned by the international director of JRS.

The next phase of my life led me as a facilitator and organizational consultant living in Rome to work with women and men in apostolic communities on their organizational development. Together, we designed skills and processes for assemblies, faith-filled leadership and membership programs, and large system events known as general chapters. Above all, we wanted to effect change through small base groups in local villages and contexts. My journeys extended at that time to Namibia, Lesotho, South Africa, Mauritius, Kenya, Senegal, the Gambia, Central Africa, Rwanda, Burkina Faso, Cameroon, and Nigeria. In Asia, we worked in Thailand, Taiwan, Indonesia, Philippines, India,

Korea, and Sri Lanka. How much I learned from women and men in all these countries and situations! However, this work with the communities felt more solid than with JRS because nearly always, we worked with the international leadership team of the religious congregation who travelled with me and their communities were not always fleeing war and poverty in the same way. This assured a continuation and implementation of the new learning. I believe this is more effective for sustainability and the assurance of a follow-through to the work done. Besides, it was funded by the communities so there was a healthy desire to use what had been not only learned but paid for! In the light of the growing awareness of the climate crisis and the amount of damage aviation does to the environment I am convinced now that international congregations and organizations need to find another way to engage across the world. This is a big challenge but one that must be faced urgently for the sake of the common good and the survival of the planet.

Another Opportunity

As the work developed in Rome, and the organization known as Faith and Praxis for Global Leadership developed, we started a five-module International Leadership Development Program for the International Congregational Leaders, who had their headquarters there. Their outreach with their international teams extended to many countries. Initially, the staff of the program were members of either the Craighead Institute in Glasgow or the Grubb Institute of Behavioural Studies, in London. When the five international leaders who were participants in Rome asked Faith and Praxis to consider going to Africa to run a similar program, we accepted enthusiastically. This gave us the opportunity not only of facilitating or consulting to groups but also of working in depth with a limited number of participants. With further training, some of these participants eventually have become colleagues and staff members in Africa in their own right. We were three to travel—one from Scotland, one from Germany, and myself from Italy. In Uganda, we had a friend and colleague who had previously been in Rome as an international leader of an organization totally committed to Africa. She had previously worked in Uganda for thirty years, including during the Amin regime, and was a wonderful resource to us because of her contacts and local knowledge. The first leadership program took place in Uganda followed by the Training the Trainers program—an in-depth program geared to the formation of future staff in their own culture. From Uganda, we extended into Burkina Faso, Kenya, Ghana, and Rwanda in my time as Director. Today, teams of mainly African associates, continue in Tanzania and Benin.

Immaculate Nakato SMR from Uganda
working with a group in Nairobi

CHAPTER 2

The Gold of the History and Mystery of Life

Experience and Experience!

Some fundamental experiences have shaped my life. Each person working with groups in different countries of Africa and Asia have their own core experiences that have led them to where they are today. For me, the backdrop is firstly the experience of belonging to an international community, the second, a question from a colleague, and the third a conversation with an African woman.

Firstly, the community is where I belong and is a permanent feature until today. My community of the Faithful Companions of Jesus is truly international. From entering into it, I immediately experienced this internationality. I lived with five nationalities in the first experience of community. When I was studying, I was living in a community of eight nationalities, with five different languages and eight different cultures. This was a great basic training for working internationally in later years. However, two other experiences intersected with this core experience, which added significance and brought about change for me. The second was in the form of a *question from a colleague* with whom I was consulting after finishing as a training officer in the Christian Worker Movement. Obviously, in me was the question of what to do next, but I was awakened by his question: 'Do you have a dream?' I often wonder at the importance and providence of the right question at the right time. In addition, what would have happened if I had not faced up to the fact that I indeed did have a dream? The question unleashed an energy and plethora of desires that had been simmering inside me because of my five years with the Christian Worker Movement but which I had not articulated. 'Desire' is a fundamental element of the spirituality of St Ignatius, linked to discernment and the way God is calling us and shaping our life. That day, I gave expression to it and claimed the call, within my community call, to found an institute where people could really grapple with the main issues they are struggling with in family, work, neighbourhood, and civic society. There was a thirst at that time to engage with areas of injustice, to support and work alongside the poorest of the poor in society and to develop processes with them to bring about change of heart and change in their lives. The dream of starting a more permanent institute was there, but it was many years before it was fulfilled.

Let me digress for a moment to tell you about *a third experience* that really marked my life. I was working with a community in Central Africa, facilitating an assembly of forty missionaries. The area was poor and war-torn, with another war just about to break out. In the evening, I walked on the dry, cracked earth, where absolutely nothing was growing, so food was short. On my walk, I met an elderly woman who was not part of my group. I remarked to her about the drought and how difficult life was in that area.

She looked me straight in the eye and said, 'Yes, but *it is not just the land that is dry; our hearts are dry!*' I was so moved by her evident pain but also her hope as we continued to converse and heard her say she did not need the West only to be bringing material gifts useful as they are, but she needed us to help her discover meaning and light within this dire situation. With her, I recognized her thirst for meaning, and it inflamed my desire to work at meaning with groups of people in equally dried out situations at home and abroad. I belong to a community that had education as its main work, and I recognized that development education in unstructured situations was where I belonged and to which I was missioned by my leaders.

Spirituality in Action that Has Been a Light for My Path

I am sharing some elements of spirituality as they emerge in trying to articulate the meaning of this spirituality with the experience of everyday life. The context was our faith and the desire to work with others to take up our role as citizens in society. Reflecting on the content and processes necessary, I recognized in the spirituality of St Ignatius a very significant way of moving from intensely spiritual devotions to the work of transformation of society. I am sharing here a few details in the hope that others can recognize them in their own lives and build on them.

What we learn immediately in this spirituality is the ability to recognize the importance of experience. Every one of us lives in a particular context and culture. In this spirituality, each person is invited to get in touch with where they are now—family, work, prayer, leisure, finances, citizenship—and to acknowledge the reality of what we are living. This is not evident when the reality of life is overpowering people despite all their good will. We would like to come before God with empty hands and open hearts, but for most people, life is not like this. A way needs to be found to seek relevance in everyday life—not just for the rich and powerful but for the poor and marginalized, the young and the old, the displaced and refugees. We are often full of busyness, confusions, worries, and perplexities that form the very stuff of our experience. Ignatius teaches us not to ignore these but to work with this experience for the health of our own situations and the good of humanity. He teaches us not to pretend to solve these or deny them but to acknowledge them and to integrate the sacred space of our experience with the reality of God's love and our faith in that. I love the definition once offered to me of faith that *faith is the ability to live with uncertainty.*

The risk of accepting this uncertainty and vulnerability is at the heart of the Christian message and so we began to meet in groups and reflect together as a basis for our work. The 'What can we do about it?' question, which arises in the context of social, economic, political and cultural reality, when analysed, is an opportunity to take a quantum leap from an individual spirituality to a corporate Christian responsibility for society. Ignatius painted a broad sweep of reality rather than a detailed one. The backdrop of his life and work was always the mercy and love of God.

The person who moves into this dynamic does so to bring about change, and for that, we need to move out of isolation, find likeminded people, and become part of a more organized force for change in society. Hence the importance of the small and large group and the need to develop skills necessary to work in them. What is evident is that the spirituality of St Ignatius is not a theory or a strategy but a way of life and this involves sifting our experience together and trying to deepen meaning and the consequent action. It is not the only way as the Christian worker movements and other organizations have offered different methodologies, all of which seek to address the gap between the faith we profess and the lives we live. Most people, however, do not join movements but work through the various structures of society—economic, political, ecclesial, cultural, and social—to fulfil their social and Christian commitment. Although a huge amount of intellectual work is done in this sphere, there is a dearth of practitioners able and willing to accompany people in areas that are confusing and messy. This is what our work is about both as practitioners ourselves but also in seeking to train more people to accompany and sustain small and large groups. Within these groups, we discover leaders who with more training make a significant difference, especially in Africa, in community organizations, schools, and healthcare centres.

In the early years of the Craighead Institute, we had a cohesive, skilled team of five members. We worked hard in focus groups and staff meetings to spell out for each other the main tenets of our mission and methodology. In this, we were greatly helped by a consultant in the Grubb Institute who came to some of our meetings to help us unknot some of the situations that all organizations go through in their early stages. We worked hard at taking up our roles effectively—both the struggle of it and the freedom of it. We were an enthusiastic group of people with different backgrounds and all with a commitment to working in the poorest areas. Without these colleagues, I would not have survived the many obstacles we were to meet along the way.

Having a dream and experience was not enough to provide plain sailing in the founding of an Institute at the service of the training and facilitation of these groups. We met many roadblocks on the way. The first was not so much an obstacle as a lack of understanding of some members of my own community. I was trained as a teacher, so what was I doing moving away, even with the consent of my leaders, to live out my commitment in a different way? This difference pursued me for much of my active life though less so in the last fifteen years where, as I said, difference is now more accepted.

The next big obstacle was finance. Where would the money come from to start an institute? The dream of starting the institute had many implications, and looking back, I am glad I did not foresee all the difficulties. Because we were working in poorer areas, our fees were very low. Most of our money came from facilitation and consultancy and balanced income from the training. We also had many donors, including my own FCJ community and the Society of Jesus, who supported us in the early years of the work.

However, a split risked developing between facilitation and training. There was a feeling among some staff members that facilitation was being seen as superior to the training and some trainers wanted to charge equivalent fees for the work in the local areas. They were right in that they were working as hard as the facilitators, but all the money went into the same pot and was shared as just salaries for all, according to the norms of adult education. Another spilt that appeared was that when some new staff members joined us after the initial foundation, it was hard for them to embrace the methodology and processes that we had developed, and they wanted to include more 'spirituality' and 'counselling'. As director, I always seemed to be holding the boundaries of what we were about and was not always popular for doing so. A couple of people left quite disgruntled, but in fact, it was an opportunity for us all to examine our way of acting as an Institute and to renew our commitment to the priority of the small and large group work and a methodology for social justice in the poorer areas of society. It was also an alert as regards the amount of preparation needed for new people to join a group which is already quite cohesive. This was not a job but a commitment—a way of life.

Unexpectedly something significant happened that was another challenge in holding the organization together. When Lithuania became independent, we were invited to send a team to Kaunas to work with a large school to help the staff who had until then been under the Communist regime. The task was the same—the integration of experience and the values, belief, and faith of the participants. However, back in Glasgow, a new split appeared—this time between the team where some members were able to travel and could be away from family and community for a week at a time and those who did not want to do this or who for practical family reasons were unable to do this. I respected this and was glad others were 'holding the fort' back in Glasgow. However, I learned yet again that it is not possible to transfer experience and those of us who had travelled and experienced both joy and hardship had built up a spirit of enthusiasm and desire to fulfil a new dream with our participants in Lithuania—that of founding an Institute in Kaunas with the Jesuit community there. It still exists today. It took many visits and absences, not to mention preoccupations as we sought the funders and developed the new Institute in the centre of Kaunas.

Once we started in Lithuania, the story did not end there. We were next invited to go to Croatia and Bosnia, followed by Zimbabwe, Kenya, and various countries of Asia. Again, teams worked extensively in Zagreb and Sarajevo just as the war was finishing and refugees were everywhere. They were also countries coming out of Communism, so there was need for a lot of group work and training to enable families and communities to talk about their experiences and try to move on—literally in many cases. Again, the work was demanding and risky at times, but there was a joy and challenge in being part of helping others discover new meaning. We ourselves were being exposed all the time to new experiences and hence new learning despite the suffering and hardship in which we worked. We were aware that we were so dependent on the local people to take the work forward once we had left.

In the original document, written before we started the institute of Life and Faith, it was envisaged that the institute would be ecumenical and international, but we had never imagined how that would be. Over the next years, we continued and developed strongly as an organization despite any obstacles we had faced. The staff did not travel with me very often to Africa or Asia, as I had been asked by the director of Jesuit Refugee Service to be a consultant to him as he visited the teams in Africa and Asia. Later, still as director of Craighead Institute, I did an organizational review for JRS International, travelling to many African countries, including Liberia, Ivory Coast, Burundi, Rwanda, Kenya, Zimbabwe as well as several countries of Asia including Sri Lanka, India, Thailand, the Philippines and Indonesia.

Time to Move On

Through all this, the institute needed a new phase and a new director. I had been there for sixteen years, and we had often discussed how to find a new director. When I moved to Rome in

2003 to work at the International Centre of JRS, a new director was appointed. Sadly, it did not work out for someone to take up a role which by then was quite complex. The question also of moving from founder to the next director is never easy, and it took several years before the institute stabilized again.

What I have been doing here in this chapter is just giving you a little bit of background from where the training, research, and consultancy evolved. The methodology and processes are the same but were greatly enriched by having an international team working in Rome. I did not intend to start another organization or institute. Faith and Praxis for Global Leadership was simply started in Rome to provide the legal and financial framework for some training programs and consultancy. These were offered to the leadership of international teams of women and men who had their headquarters in Rome. It was also a much looser structure, as the team was dispersed over several countries of Europe and it was not so easy to meet and work in depth together. At Craighead, everyone was salaried, but in Faith and Praxis, each one earned their living by the work they did and as associates, they committed to contributing a percentage of their earnings to the upkeep of the new organization. After some time, we were integrated into the British Charity of my own community, based in England. However, it is within Faith and Praxis for Global Leadership that I first met as participants in the leadership program African colleagues, who are now currently or are soon to be active in Africa. They followed not only the five-module leadership program but also a three-module Training the Trainers program.

CHAPTER 3

The Gold of Creative Emerging Newness

What Is Faith and Praxis?

The faith I am talking about is not about a body of theology or ethics but the faith of Abraham: 'It was by faith that Abraham set out … without knowing where he was going' (Hebrews 11:8).

When I talk about *faith*, I mean the willingness to live with uncertainty and to face a future that is not our right and is unknown. The intercultural world we live in today is challenging all people of faith to deepen reflection and to articulate their beliefs with sensitivity to the belief systems of others. Contemporary life calls us to express our search for meaning in practical ways, respectful of all the great faiths and none.

By *praxis*, I mean holding the tension between theory and experience, the practical application of the gospel message in the heart of the intercultural developing world. In the Christian context, this engages the believer in all aspects of society to sift through our practice by rigorous discernment and to seek coherence in our values and activities. This desire is what motivated myself and my colleagues, and it was to this end we embarked on a robust approach to training in Rome for the executive groups of international organizations who have their headquarters there.

Addressing the Gap between Experience and Faith

The mission of the Craighead Institute in Glasgow was exactly this: to work with groups of people in many different sectors of society who were struggling to bring about social change in their area and who were for the most part Christians. Sometimes the two aspects did not seem to fit together. Providentially, not long after we started the institute, I met Maureen McGuigan and with her, we designed a program for the groups, elements of which still exist today, so many years later. It was called the Social and Pastoral Ministry program, later renamed the Integrating Life and Faith Program.

This first colleague in Glasgow wrote the program with me and we agreed on five things:

- The spirituality of St Ignatius is a good vehicle to work through and accessible to all.
- We wanted to work with disadvantaged groups in bringing about social justice and learn from and make practical the social teaching of all the churches.
- We acknowledged that this would be done by us going to the participants as well as the participants also coming to the centre.
- We would work consistently through small and large groups using the principles of development education and group theory.
- The institute would be ecumenical and international.

Throughout all of this work, the challenge was to enable people to move from a personal approach to spirituality that enabled them to grow in their love and understanding of God to a spirituality connected to the transformation of society.

It was out of this experience in Glasgow, later extended to Lithuania, Croatia, and Bosnia that it was logical to develop the first Diploma for Facilitation and Consultancy in Craighead Institute. This continued in Rome in an amended way a few years later. In these programs, we gathered staff from the Grubb Institute of Behavioural Studies in London and the Craighead Institute for the Integration of Life and Faith in Glasgow. Eventually, new staff of Faith and Praxis, having completed their training in the Grubb Institute, took over the development of the program as it continues in Rome until now.

In the first place in Rome, we opened a leadership program with the cosmic walk—the first movements of creation noticing and contemplating the interconnectedness of all things. This was followed by a presentation on strands of leadership that from experience we believed were most pertinent in international communities at that time. These strands became the basis of the program that was delivered over two years and remained the fundamental basis for the curriculum for a further four years. Obviously, the world has evolved, the program is redesigned as the context changes, and much is done online.

The following are some of the strands that from our experience surfaced repeatedly in different contexts. These strands come from reflecting on the experiences and connecting them to each other in different continents and in different organizations. They surface repeatedly and are still relevant today.

Faith-filled Leadership in a Time of Unknowing

It is so true that in organizations and apostolic communities, we are no longer clear about where we are going! Strategies written and rewritten are being torn up as the tectonic plates of the organization and of the earth move under them! We are today in a crisis, at a balancing point between extinction in some cases and having the courage to engage in transformation. There is a bigger issue: How can we talk about leadership without acknowledging the crisis and suffering of our planet of which we are part? The participants in the program are travelling to many different countries and are seeing for themselves the devastating effects of climate change in droughts, famines, floods, hurricanes and violence as people fight to share minimum resources. Covid-19, the effects of climate change and the pandemic have totally changed our perspective.

There is more to it than that as we reflect on ecology and leadership and that is about raising awareness that each one of us is responsible for the care of the earth. One day, when I was working in one country, I noticed water leaking out of a pipe. When I challenged this I was told, 'It doesn't matter because we have plenty of water now.' However, we can no longer look at our world from a very limited and local perspective. We need to connect the different parts of our ecosystem and of our organization. Ecology forces us to think about the global world in which we exercise our leadership and membership today. Only then do most of us consider the interconnectedness between plants, animals and their environments and the effects of our care of them on the world. So too with our organizations. Ecology teaches us that we cannot sustain ourselves alone as the environment is interconnected. It is so important for us at a basic level to understand for example that if we waste water in one part of the world, this has an impact on another part of the world. In damaging one part of the ecosystem, we have an effect on others. This concept holds true also for our organizations and the way we manage our resources and are sensitive to the needs of the planet as well as our own. Individualism militates against this approach, and communities are challenged to put ecological processes at the heart of the work. Too often, internal and rightly pressing administrative issues work against this, and yet the overriding factor is that we are citizens of the earth with one human story.

Because we are all interconnected, being members in a system means getting to know the connectedness of one another's stories. It means understanding one another not just on the surface but also from the inside out. Each one's story was the resource of every participant in the program and one that we sought to share through the small group work. Through these stories, we were listening to the truth of experience, including the tough truth that always flows from stories that raise issues of vulnerability, forgiveness, and reconciliation.

A Systemic Leadership—A Leadership That Makes Connections

As a staff team, we were deeply influenced in our work by the training we received as organizational consultants and role analysts at the Grubb Institute of Behavioural Studies. The Grubb Institute as such no longer exists but the body of thinking lives on in many organizations around the world including Faith and Praxis for Global Leadership. The basis of that training was a rigorous approach to the understanding of the theory of systems and the interconnectedness of all things. This was a great gift to me that I was able to share at a time when it is so easy for organizations to become dysfunctional and fragmented because they do not see the interconnectedness of all things. The concept of *systemic* was new for many participants, and they often confused it with *systematic* which is quite different and more linear. In our fragmented world, connectedness of peoples and connectedness within the organization is crucial so that we do not contribute to the disintegration experienced at times around us. A leadership that makes connections is a systemic leadership— based on the theory of systems and giving a framework of clarity of purpose, boundaries, and roles to our organizations. A system can be defined simply as 'activities within a boundary'. The basis of our work was that of 'wholeness' in the sense that the whole is more than the sum of the parts of the organizations. The great advantage we had in the Rome program was that all the participants were actively involved in leading and managing large international organizations at this time, and their experience was a great resource with which to work. It was a resource to themselves and a resource to each other.

The skills of systemic leadership helped to clarify and transform the connectedness of each part with the whole. In this strand, I recognized we needed to work together not just to collaborate but to co-create together. This raises huge implications for the understanding of leadership and membership and of the place of authority in the organizations.

A Leadership of Discontinuity

This is very typical of most organizations though it is not always acknowledged. How often we ask ourselves how long we can keep our organization going. Are we going to survive economically? Will we attract new members? What do we need to say to each other today to help us to move on? What if we are dying out and no longer serve the purpose for which we were created? This moving on may not be physical but a set of internal 'rules' written by ourselves for ourselves or sometimes even just ways of being that mean 'we have always done it like this'.

Discontinuity, when acknowledged by leadership, nurtures imagination, faith and discernment and above all creativity. This is the type of leadership that encourages adherence to a different future within the organization and reflects and dialogues with the membership to discern what that could look like. This is the leadership and membership that embraces the unknown—that risks not knowing where the road will lead but is sure of the providence of God accompanying us on the journey. It is an opportunity for new growth when the unexpected happens to us.

I remember working in Sri Lanka not long before the tsunami. We were working on projects where money had been raised for some fishing boats and nets for the local fishermen who were displaced during the war. Then, when the tsunami came, all this was washed away, and we were back where we started. What I noticed was not just the resilience of the people as they reconstructed their lives but how they were able to do it differently. The projects were stronger afterwards as were the people who had surmounted the disaster and struggled together. These are the sort of events that really help us to see we can change. We do not need to stay where we are. Of course, most of life is not like that, but the universe is producing change dynamics that urge us to respond in a new and creative way and not be washed away as irrelevant. Sometimes, the organization will be washed away or will die by choice, as it is no longer needed in the context.

The leadership of discontinuity allows us to think the unthinkable—even if at times it takes courage to surmount much tension in the expression of it. People who are in touch with this experience can discover new ways of seeing into the heart of things and can often be disappointed by the heaviness of the institution in which they find themselves. The work done during a module that focused on this was the most creative of all and in the evaluations was named as a turning point in the program. It was so relevant to where participants and teams were finding themselves. From each other, they found a new language to articulate their concerns and to know they were connected to a scenario that is so much bigger than their own. So in the program, we worked together to explore less rigid structures.

A Leadership of Flexibility and Spirals

This is an exploration of the leadership that is working to erode long-outdated models—models of squares and angles, rigid forms of being in organizations that have a linear model and an ongoing plan in which the unexpected is seen as an inconvenience rather than an opportunity for new growth. The type of leadership required today is one that embraces and includes what previously may not have been thinkable. It is a flexible approach, not tied down by decisions and strategies designed years before! New imaginative and creative ways of seeing into the heart of things enable us to embrace a spiral dynamic and have an openness to let go of preconceived models. Violence, war, and ecological disasters have created new scenarios in which we live and which our organizations serve. The very experience of leading them invites us to take risks and go beyond the safe parameters of tradition. Many years ago, I was asked as an organizational consultant to design a ten-year strategic plan with some organizations. A few years later, people were asking for five-year plans, then two-years, and the last one I did with a group was for six months renewable. Life is moving too fast, and so any planning needs to be open, reversible, and flexible. This can be scary, yes, but it can also be exciting. It keeps us alive and creative. Where it can fall down is when it is done by a few for others to implement! Today, most thinking people want to be involved in the process and decision-making, and this demands a lot from leaders and members in an organization if they take this seriously.

Maria Pilar Benavente Serrano

Prophetic Leadership

This leadership creates the deep ground of reflection and space for discernment and action in organizations that today are buffeted by the waves of change. Prophetic leadership goes beyond what we know; it engages with the drama of our times as found in the political, ecclesial, cultural, economic and social context as also it engages with the poetry, drama, and music of our world; prophetic leadership has the ability to express itself in a new and different language—a language that is heard, not ignored, perceived by action and welcomed and able to work with others to bring about a new creation. Sometimes we think that prophets are special people for special places for special times. Some of them are. Surprisingly enough, we probably have more prophets in our own time than we ever had. This type of leadership is a leadership that is not daunted by the amount of institutional change that we are required to make in our context today. We are neither daunted nor frightened by it. We see it is there, and we work with it in an interconnected way to make a difference in areas of injustice and poverty. The drama of the rich/poor divide is being lived out in our time as we witness the unjust distribution of resources.

The communities we were working with were all committed to social justice, and it was a theme that each one was deeply concerned to find ways to enter into this dynamic movement. Life can be hard for everyone, rich and poor, for very different reasons, but the voice of the prophet in leadership is there to mobilize members to make a noise and represent the injustices before public and private authorities. Sadly, many organizations get so obsessed with their own internal problems and administration, and they forget that if some of them are no longer relevant to society they should phase out. This is very painful to acknowledge. Prophetic leadership is informed by the voices of the poor, the voices of the suffering, and too often, we nod to this reality from the comfort of our own security and privilege. As Christians, this reality is deeply impacted by the words of the Old Testament prophets and the gospel.

Prophetic leadership is a leadership that challenges us to participation and inclusion as we work together to dissolve barriers—some local, some international. Many communities already have a voice in the UN or in other organizations specifically created for social justice. We live in a global world and can no longer think Africa, Asia, and Europe. Every place is interconnected, and we need to learn to look deeply into this and grow relationships and relatedness across these peace networks and collaborate across many NGOs and justice and peace networks.

Leadership and Theological Reflection

Some organizations can become stuck in institutionalized theology. This is often a theology of morals and ethics, of dogmas. However, there is another expression —that of people 'doing theology' in their local contexts and not waiting for the 'experts'. This is a leadership that goes beyond the traditional routes, that walks the walk with people of all faiths and cultures and does theological reflection on the way. This leadership is both prophetic and biblical and is constantly making the links between life and faith. Leadership is prophetic when we reflect and break open the word of God together within the context of our times and in communication with other faiths and when we share our wisdom, our learning and understanding with each other. In this way, we learn from each one. I discovered that if I heard the scriptures read on the twentieth floor of a block of flats in Scotland, or in the African bush, I was hearing it differently than when I was sitting in a church or cathedral listening to it. The Word is contextual. 'Blessed are the poor in spirit' has a different impact when sitting among the poor and listening to that text than when I hear it read out in a church in Europe. Most organizations are buffeted by the waves of change. Let us face it—we are all buffeted! However, to do theology does not require that we are all theologians but that we learn to make the links between the faith we profess and the experience we are living.

A Program for International Leaders

This ability to make the links between experience and faith is a central dynamic of the program that took place firstly in Rome in 2005 and was formalized as part of Faith and Praxis in 2011. It built on experience both in the Integrating Life and Faith program in Glasgow and on the work done in the Grubb Institute. The skills and reflections we did together were weaved to give a sense of re-appropriation of the mission and purpose of not just the organizations but called for a renewed understanding of leadership and membership. I put the two latter together because there is no leadership without members. The context of the program was that of faith, economy, society, local politics, and culture in our world of today. A key concept underpinned everything: the experience of the participants of the program was the key to greater learning and the most important resource that participants shared with each other.

CHAPTER 4

Gold Melted and Transformed

Education Service and Representation

Experience and knowledge is not enough. The three well-tried elements of an apostolic group in the Christian Worker Movements are education, service, and representation or advocacy. Certainly, within the programs, there is a large element of *education*—development education within local contexts and cultures. To name a few of the themes explored—cultural diversity, and difference; the local and global aspects of organization; the meaning of internationality and the value of nationality; group and leadership theory, the difference between a centralized organization and a systemic one leading to an integrated approach to leadership and membership; the evolving understanding of authority and power; and conflict and confrontation. Because the process was alive, the needs of the participants were taken into account in the program we created together.

As regards *service*, this was not an issue with many participants because the service of others is at the heart of our lives in communities. In fact, the struggle was to prevent service of the poor and vulnerable becoming unhealthy activism and a working *for* people rather than *with* people. Sometimes members have an unhealthy attitude of preferring to do the work themselves rather than train others to do it, but an element of the spirituality of St Ignatius is to work with the 'multipliers'—that is, working to enable others to do as we do, not holding on to positions and power through control. As we worked at the integration of life and faith, we were constantly reviewing the projects through discernment with a view to sustainability for the future. It was important, too, to let the leaders emerge and develop their programs and community lifestyles according to local culture and context.

The third element of the apostolic group is that of *advocacy and representing* the needs of the local people before public and private authorities. Sometimes, the people suffering the injustice could endanger their own lives or the lives of others by speaking out. As individuals, they are often not heard. At their request they need others to advocate for them and represent these needs before the UN or other powerful organizations who could give voice to their experience. At a local level, it means gathering the experience of the downtrodden and formulating it in such a way that it could be heard. This is not easy, but the social justice aspect of the training gave rise to questions and exclamations about the injustice we uncovered as we worked. In one small group meeting in a deprived area of London, the women there spoke about how they had to make their way home from working late in restaurants or cinemas, but the street lighting was broken, and there had been many muggings in the area. Individually, several women had represented this, but nothing happened. The local authority unfortunately seemed to have other priorities besides

Discerning the Gold in Human Experience

the safety of these women! Together, they decided to represent the issue as a group. Three members went to the council offices to present the request for new street lighting, handed over the signed letter from the other members, and were able to express the fear being experienced on those streets to the authorities. This had been well prepared with the representatives beforehand with the other members of the group and so and they made their points clearly. The street lighting was mended within the week! The power of the small group!

Advocacy can be exercised in small effective ways to bring about a more just situation. It can also be done on a much bigger scale to draw attention to a political injustice. During one of the wars in Burundi, the people had been displaced from their homes and were more or less prisoners on top of the hills surrounding Bujumbura, the capital. While there on JRS work, the international director of Jesuit Refugee Service, the advocacy officer, and I managed to get through the armed security, and we set off up the hills to see for ourselves the terrible situation of deprivation in which the people were living. There we gathered information and photos and learned about the oppression and illness, including seeing people lying on the ground dying of typhoid. That evening, the international director left for Geneva to visit the United Nations. His object was to share the information about the displaced and the conditions in which they were being forced to live to bring this situation to the notice of the international community. Twenty-four hours later, the media were broadcasting the situation in Burundi, including some of our photos. In this way the international community was alerted to the situation. This story illustrates that the Burundians were powerless to move at the time, held prisoners on the hills, but others could discretely gather the information and bring it to the attention of public authority. Advocacy has many facets, some small and possible for all and some political, as the above example demonstrates.

Robust Processes for Transformation

For small groups to work effectively, sound methodologies are necessary. There are many different approaches, but the focus of the ones in the countries where we worked drew heavily on a *social pastoral process* of experience, social analysis, theological reflection and action. It was important for us to work with a methodology that was well known and accepted internationally. It was also one used frequently in social justice groups and projects.

Experience was the basis of the work in the groups. This was not an academic program but a practical one. Consequently, the groups could be happily mixed ability—some with doctorates and some with minimum schooling. It did not matter because each one came with their own experience, and this was the particular resource they had to offer. This was offered by sharing stories and experiences of daily life and work and applying the methodologies to them.

Social Analysis

The UN Declaration on Human Rights and the seventeen Sustainable Development Goals inspired this analytic approach. We reflected on these through the social teaching of the Catholic Church. This teaching embraces, among others, the themes of the life and dignity of the human person, their rights and responsibilities, the option for the poor and vulnerable and solidarity and the care of God's creation. When Cardinal Joseph Cardijn, the son of a Belgian miner, founded the Young Christian Workers, he presented three truths to the young workers.

The *truth of faith*: that all of us are created and called to live with dignity in the very circumstances in which we find ourselves.

The *truth of reality* is that some unjust situations in which people are living, whether it be areas such as working conditions, housing, or unemployment, undermine their ability to live with dignity and demonstrate the injustices often being endured.

The *truth of method*: Cardijn was concerned about the gap between the faith professed in churches on a Sunday and what the young men and women were forced to live during the week. In response to this, he founded the organization of the Young Christian Workers. This organization flourishes today in many countries, and the methodology is used in hundreds of groups. Cardijn offered a methodology to address the synthesis needed so that the young workers were enabled to work through a method known today internationally as *see, judge, act*. Week by week, the young people shared in groups the facts of their experience—not theory but the reality. They analysed the experience in the light of the context, the gospel, and the social teaching of the church. Both greatly support the dignity and rights of workers. In the light of their discoveries together, they decided what action to take. Action for Cardijn was not taking on more activity but rather addressing the injustices they had discovered in the social analysis. Together the group agreed in what small or big way how they could respond together to the injustices the analysis had uncovered.

This social analysis was further enriched by introducing participants to a systemic analysis of the organizations in which they were living and working. The interconnectedness of each part with the whole widened their perspective.

Linking faith, values, and beliefs with experience

Following the social analysis, time was spent on reflection arising from the link between life and faith. This is known in some circles as theological reflection, but for our purposes, we did this in a very practical way.

At the heart of the spirituality of St Ignatius is the practice of discernment. Many people think of decision-making when they hear the word discernment, but the work we did in the groups at that time encouraged participants to see *discernment as a way of life*. Together, we explored the meaning of discernment linked to our deepest desires in relation to God and different aspects of our beliefs. This was the first stance of discernment—being clear about the facts of the situations described. We contextualized this using the experiences everyone had brought into the group in terms of the social, economic, political, cultural, and ecclesial situations they were facing. Then we looked at the areas that prevented participants living with true interior freedom. Having named these, we sifted the experiences in terms of what was bringing us into deeper faith, hope, and love as a basis for transformation and what was leading us into attitudes that are more negative. Always underlying this was the urge to make decisions and so we outlined a process of decision-making. Such a process would only be used for important issues and was not a method for every day.

This process can take place over several weeks or months. The decision to be made is clearly outlined, and those who enter into a discernment process need to be prepared by disposing themselves to be open to the result, even if it is not my choice. Listening attentively to all initial opinions is very important.

This is followed by a time of thorough fact-finding and research. It is important to clarify at this stage who is the discerning body and who has the responsibility for the final decision. Is it a group or an individual? The people most affected by the decision are essential to the integrity of the process. Cardijn always said if a group is discussing the needs of coalminers, then the miners have to be there! If the leadership is discussing the needs of members, the concerned members need to be part of the discussion. This reverses the idea of leadership giving directions and membership following. There needs to be thorough consultation with those whose lives are going to be affected.

The decision making body focuses the decision in the context of the Word of God as experienced in the *text* of the Bible, the *context* of the community, and the current events, including the *facts* already gathered and the *experience* of each one concerned.

Consultation is made with appropriate bodies and individuals, and following this, the findings are shared with all involved. Consultation is not decision-making. Consultation feeds into the decision-making. There follows then an extended time of reflection, dialogue, and contemplation to give everyone time to weigh up the findings. At this stage, a list of possible options regarding the issue is drawn up. It is important to write these options down and share them with others to ensure that every person's preference is recorded and the implications are taken into account.

The discerning group live with each option in turn. They explore in faith and prayer their deepest feelings in relation to the option, and the inner process is noted and later shared.

Discernment is a choice between two alternatives that are both good. All participants take time to prepare their hearts and minds to arrive at the freedom of letting go of their own preference if it is not the one chosen. This is demanding, and requires a certain amount of dialogue, prayer, and inner freedom.

It may seem obvious, but sometimes, the discerning body gets so lost in the process of consultation that they never seem to be able to reach a decision, which, of course, is an essential conclusion to the process! A healthy time scale can help here, even if it needs to be extended along the way. In our evolving world no decision is forever but it needs to be the best decision we can make at the time.

Action and the Review of Life

Action and apostolic activity are not the same thing. The Young Christian Worker movement focuses on the review of life. This is an integral part of the methodology for the local groups. In this meeting, the participants examine the action to be taken in the light of the context and the gospel. They also plan how to respond to the injustices they have discovered in the social analysis. It can be something very simple like preparing an agenda for a future event or something more public like taking part in a mass protest. At the next meeting, this is shared with one another in a spirit of accountability and gathering of learning. In religious communities, sometimes a review of life is seen by some members as control, but the accountability being asked for can be related more to the mission each one is carrying out on behalf of the whole organization. In this way, we can gather the wisdom together for the greater development and service into the future.

CHAPTER 5

Gold Tried in the Furnace of Life

Praxis Events and Organizational Role Analysis

Both the Praxis events and the sessions of Organizational Role Analysis were initially designed by the Grubb Institute of Behavioural Studies. With staff from the Grubb Institute, we developed these as essential aspects of all programs in Rome and in Africa.

What was noticeable, as individual leaders or teams of different congregations worked separately with me in the context of their own organizations, was that they had all more or less similar organizational issues. To this end, it seemed that it would be more beneficial if the leaders and members could work with each other across organizations. We created an open space once a week for anyone to drop into the offices of the International Union of Superiors General, where they took part in a Praxis session of two hours. These sessions consisted of one person presenting a situation related to the role that individual held at the time. The presenter worked with the consultant for twenty minutes. The other members of the group observed, and they were encouraged to work with the feelings and experiences that the particular issue raised for themselves. No one was invited to give advice but rather to work later with the consultant to analyse the persons, roles, contexts, and systems involved in the issues presented and their own experience in listening to the presenter. In the meantime, the presenter listened to the conversation but remained silent. After another fifteen to twenty minutes, the presenter shared how they now saw their issue and what their next step might be in the situation in which they were involved.

Within the two-hour time scale in the Praxis events, there was time for one more person to present, but participants acknowledged that even if they did not present their own issue, they were learning much that was relevant to themselves in their role by listening to other participants and participating in the analysis.

When Faith and Praxis for Global Leadership was founded in 2011, the five module leadership program continued, based on the strands of leadership as mentioned previously. However, organizational role analysis became the most important aspect of the program. In the early years of its development, Maria Pilar Benavente Serrano, joined the staff and immediately trained in the Grubb Institute. She was named coordinator of the Africa Programs and staff member of the leadership programs in Rome. Her contribution was invaluable, as she herself had lived in Africa and had also been general leader of her congregation, the Sisters of Our Lady of Africa.

In the program, everyone was given the opportunity to analyse their role in the context of the issues they were facing. An outstanding approach developed by the Grubb Institute was 'Organization in the Mind'. This consisted of asking the individual or the team to draw their organization and not to put any words on this drawing. Some amazing learning took place in these sessions as members of teams explored how differently they all perceived the same organization, both consciously and unconsciously.

Once the drawings were displayed and commented on by the others and then by the designers themselves, it became obvious that all the images were good but they lacked an organizational model to hold them all together. It was then that we focused on a systemic model of organization, placing the leadership on the outside boundary and thus providing space for others to manage their own role. The outside boundary is held by the purpose or mission of the organization, for that is what the leadership is called on to develop and articulate. This clarity of purpose requires a lot of work at times. The overall mission unifies the organization, it motivates the members, and it clarifies what the organization is for, both for the members themselves and for other organizations in the environment. Understandably, different cultural contexts affect the way organizations are perceived. This can be dramatic in an international team. It is also a great richness in terms of learning and experience.

We learned much from the way participants drew themselves in role in their organization. Some of the learning was a revelation to themselves and to other members of the teams. One man drew himself with a jagged line in black down the middle of the picture. From that ensued a discussion about how to take up a role as a part-time member of the organization. Another leader drew herself in a corner of the picture, looking out defensively at the other members. Some drew plants or trees with no roots or pictures with or without people or cultural context. These are just some examples from which learning could be drawn—depicting both inner and outer processes and often a person said at the end of the process that they never knew they saw their role like that.

Christine Anderson fcj handing over to Emili Turu Rofes, fms, as Director of Faith and Praxis in January 2019

Towards an Integrated Model of Organization

It emerges in our work that people see the same organization differently. For some, it is very much hierarchical, with the leader on the top, with some rigid structures of governance. For others, one could almost call their model an example of an open field—no boundaries at all and people wandering in and out as they wished and even using the system for their own purposes. Some were in the phase of a more collaborative model, based on discernment, with the leaders in the centre and satellites in orbit around them. In Faith and Praxis, we designed a model known as the Integrated Model of Leadership. In the integrated model, the boundaries define the difference that the organization makes in the context in which it is working in its many locations. It is the boundaries that hold the mission of the organization and give unity, motivation, and clarity to what the organization is about. The position of the leadership is on the outside boundary facilitating the mission of the whole organization and delegating appropriate authority to the parts. All these parts have the same mission.

The boundaries enable the organization to interact clearly with the context and other national and international bodies. They are flexible and do not set themselves in stone like barriers. An organization that has barriers or is too rigid is moribund, as it can't breathe to enable new life and creativity to thrive. In the integrated model, everyone is part of the whole; there are no first-class and second-class members, as each one is carrying out their role on behalf of the mission. The interconnectedness of the members is through the common mission which is the constant point of reference. The authority in this model consists in taking up one's role in relation to the mission. This is important because it puts the emphasis not just in relation to the status of leader and but on the importance of each one, staff and members. However a big issue is always in relation to authority. Where does the authority lie in such a model? The authority comes through inner authority and understanding of participating in the mission. It is consequently connected to the integrity with which each one is carrying out the mission in their assigned role.

The integrated model is a very inclusive model, as each one develops a deeper understanding of the overall mission and their part in it. Although the roles are different, the mission is the same. Of course, this implies the mutual trust of the leaders and the staff or members. Just as the leader is working to the mission of the organization, so are the staff or members, including voluntary helpers. The overall mission of an international organization is the same but today there needs to be just so much room for the people in the different countries to contextualize it in their particular context and culture.

With a clear identity, the organization is more defined in its context, and people both internationally and locally can engage with the organization as such and not just individuals within it. Interestingly, participants discover that with a clearer profile, it is easier for people to both join the organization and also to leave it. This is because the mission is recognized from outside the organization as well as within.

Analysis of an Organization

Sometimes larger groups want to deepen further and to analyse the whole organization. This is a much more detailed process and includes an exploration of many aspects. For example, the need to really spell out, rediscover, and articulate some basic convictions.

This required an exploration of the guiding values, beliefs, and principles emerging as part of the culture of the organizations and included as a way of helping the reflection to move forward. Communities, regions, and districts that connect multiple parts of the international organization can significantly enhance their capabilities for profound individual and organizational change by cross-organizational collaboration. This latter is very difficult for groups that are used to thinking only of their own geographical boundary. Today, the concept of the global world is an important factor in organizational development.

An analysis of an organization is an analysis of the systems that make up the organization, which includes existing structures of the whole system and the sub-systems. Structures do not have a life of their own but are closely connected to values and context, to leadership and membership, and to resources of finance and personnel. All these areas are taken into account in the analysis. So often, as consultants, we were asked to help an organization restructure. There is no quick way to do this, as structures are only one of the ways that the mission of the organization affects the context. To restructure well, most of the work needs to be done with the leaders and members together to understand the changing face of the mission in the light of expansion and diminishment. The new structures are a response to that and also cannot be achieved without transparency of financial resources and personnel

It is helpful at this stage to have an agreed-upon understanding of the organization in the mind and heart. This is important for each one, and dialoguing what we are willing to cede to each other to move on can lead not just to resolution but to conflict, where there is no common ground regarding the values of the organization. Conflict arises when there is a difference of values.

Organizational Role Analysis

This is an essential exploration of how roles are being taken up on behalf of the organization through the ministry assigned to each one in the service of the mission or purpose of the organization. This is a privileged opportunity for renewal so that each one's role is valued in the context of the mission. It is amazing how often this is not felt by the members. Some even express it by saying they don't count! It is not an easy moment, as each one explores their connectedness not just to the persons but also to the context and the systems and the mission of the whole.

As we analyse the organization, it is normal that issues of authority and power arise that call forth a renewed understanding of discernment. Also, the impact of context on the organization and the difference that a particular organization is trying to make in the context give rise to burning issues, many of which are related to the myths, rituals, and symbols of different cultures.

An analysis of the culture, including the social, economic, political, ecclesial, and cultural contexts and their implications includes three areas:

working with difference in the same organization, a process of discontinuity for a time of change and transition and finding a new language for a new world.

No analysis is ever complete, yet it is a step towards helping the organization reflect on itself in a more objective way and move on to further analytic and theological reflection in relation to the mission and values of the organization. For example, for religious organizations, it was recognized that they are not just a business. They are an endeavour in faith to respond to God's call in today's world. Sometimes, the zeal for the latter, so evident in the variety of ministries referred to, can lead to a neglect of organizational processes, which, when understood and adhered to, can give the members ever greater freedom for mission. To this end, the analysis is an attempt to reflect on areas that could enhance the charism rather than make judgments on what is or is not helpful.

If we look at the organization as one that is continuously learning, certain similarities and differences emerge which give rise to some, not all, of the issues that need to be attended to at critical times. In the light of this, organizational role analysis sessions are encouraged for the senior executive and management team. This is an essential aspect of leadership development in Faith and Praxis and probably the most appreciated aspect of the program. It is also a way we frequently worked with large systems, assemblies, and leadership conferences.

Jim Christie SJ and Maria Pilar Msola relaxing after the leadership program in Rome

CHAPTER 6

The Gold of Transforming Roles

We come now to the whole question of taking up a role in an organization for the sake of mission. Very often, as soon as we use the word *role*, different images are conjured up by the one hearing it. 'My role' is interpreted as my job or my ministry. Or else 'my role' is identified with my status in an organization—teacher, leader, matron, senior executive. Or it could be acting in a particular role in a drama. When we talk about role in organizational analysis sessions, we are talking about an inner positioning of ourselves in relation to the organization and the context of the society around us. It is a psychological positioning of ourselves, moving from an inner understanding of 'myself in role' to an expression of it in relation to the whole organization. This is quite difficult for us to understand because of the external pressures. The greatest temptation in the Praxis events is for others to want to give advice, and yet, the understanding of taking up a role effectively is not an intellectual understanding but an inner journey that the person needs to make. The temptation, not only for participants but also for the staff working with them, is to cut corners because of the

The Gold of Transforming Roles

time pressure or their own lack of ability to stay with some of the conscious or unconscious processes that participants need to go through. Taking up a new role, for example, demands that the person has the ability to identify for themselves the systems and subsystems in which they are called to work—in other words, working at the systems and subsystems within the boundary of an organization. Some people, perhaps overly generous in nature, want to expand the boundaries with disastrous effects. I remember one team member being sent from an organization I was working with to manage a project within a certain geographical area of Africa. He was skilled and enthusiastic, and the organization had sufficient resources of personnel and finance to do this. However, his enthusiasm or ambition got out of hand, and he set up another similar, albeit good-intentioned, project in another area. There was, however, a serious difficulty—he overextended the resources both of personnel and finance, and both projects crumbled! Evidently, he was out of role and had not understood from within himself either the boundaries of the project or the system and subsystems in which he was paid to work. So, identifying the activities within the boundary is the very first exercise we need to do to be able to think about a role.

Another important aspect is that we cannot take up a role within an organization unless the mission or aim of the particular part of the system is identified. We take up a role in relation to an aim, so that really needs to be clarified. There can be a clear overall mission, but for the participants within the organization, working on behalf of the organization, both leaders and members must spell out to each other what each one is being asked to do on behalf of the whole. Sometimes, we think if we have a job description, that is enough, but unless we claim the responsibilities and activities of the position in relation to other activities in the field, the person is doomed to failure—or at least a good dose of unpopularity! So, it is really important early on, if we are joining an organization, to examine the internal and external context, including the roles of other positions and the objectives already in place.

We can't use all our skills at the same time. For example, if we speak Spanish but the working language of the system is English, we use the skill of speaking English. This is obvious for language but not so obvious for some of the other necessary skills. Sometimes, people are appointed in organizations in diminishment who don't have the skills for the work. Taking up a role demands having the competence to do so in relation to the aim. If this doesn't happen, the whole organization is weakened, and the person also becomes frustrated.

It is really important to stay in touch with the feelings, both positive and negative, that we experience as we go through these steps in the early months of a new position. Sometimes, people discover very quickly through discernment whether they are in the right position. Others thrive in the new situation, while some drag along for years producing a mediocre response to the environment because they are staying there for the salary or the status or because in a religious organization they have been requested to do so and do not want to rock the boat.

Faith-filled leadership and authority

Many of the sessions in both Praxis events and in organizational role analysis had to do with issues of authority and power in the systems in which people were working. In this chapter, I am referring particularly to religious congregations. The words authority, faith, and accountability have not come out of the air but rather are ones which we continually find ourselves working with in so many of the congregations, of both women and men, throughout the world. Why are these words so important for our times? What can they say to us that will help us to move out of the confusion and at times paralysis of apostolic religious congregations today and be ever more relevant and meaningful both to ourselves and in the wider context of society? My purpose is just to offer some reflections for dialogue and discernment for action and to show the interconnectedness between these themes.

Faith-filled leadership and membership

This is the leadership and membership we would all like to have at the heart of our lives: a leadership and membership full of faith, driven by zeal and enthusiasm in apostolic work for the kingdom, and drawn into the heart of God. Such a leadership operates not in isolation but in the context of today in the world and our congregations. There are, of course, named or elected leaders. However, all members are also called to leadership in society and in the world, although this may be expressed in different ways. Key questions for every congregation:

- How is God working through our congregation to make a difference in the contexts where we are living and working?
- How are we as leaders and members affecting the international context of the world?
- How are the people of God called, formed, and sustained in their own ministry through us?

Discerning the Gold in Human Experience

In other words, are we engaging with the world through faith-filled leadership or retreating into our own busyness and concerns?

Accountability

This is an unpopular and even negative word today, both in religious and business spheres. A religious congregation, although it has much administration, is not just a business but a faith enterprise. What does accountability mean in that context? Accountability has become an uncomfortable word for so many people because their experience of it has been one of control or checking up on the person.

When we make a commitment, as in consecrated religious life, we do become personally accountable and interested in keeping our word. Accountability has become unpopular because *it has become linked to authority and leadership instead of to mission and ministry.* It has become more about the person and the authority figure and less about the role of that person in relation to the mission of the congregation. Accountability is about engagement and commitment to the ministry and the way of life to which each one of us has been mandated or sent on mission. Through accountability, the new wisdom and learning is shared and is important information for the ongoing discernment of the organization. Sadly, because of the pace of life, it is difficult to keep a balance of reflection and praxis in many cases.

A new way of talking about responsibility and accountability is evolving—a way which recognizes and respects each one, whatever he or she, leader or member, is doing on behalf of the whole congregation.

Some organizational consultants say that a large percentage of change initiatives fail because leaders and members do not set up the process for evaluation and accountability—it is left to good will or forgotten about in a very busy life. Often there are no clear expectations articulated, and accountability conjures up negative connotations largely because people experience accountability as something done to them or a way of controlling them.

I would also like to suggest that *accountability is less a word than a process.* It is not threatening when it is well designed and collaboratively designed. It can emphasize growth, not judgment, and be aligned more closely not just with the needs of the congregation and its mission but also with the impact the context is having on the ministry of the person-in-role.

And so with aspects of authority, we explore authority in relation to our role in the congregation as it concerns the mission and try to unbind it from the narrow perspective of being linked only to the superiors or leaders in communities and all the projections that go with that. It is our engagement and commitment that keeps us going, that links faith, authority, and accountability and helps to give meaning and purpose to our lives through our ministries.

Faith-filled leadership at a time of discontinuity

The usual models of leadership that come from the world of management do not really fit the experience of consecrated life, although they may provide some valuable assistance. Faith-filled leadership is something quite different because it challenges us at the very core of our commitment to Christ. At this time in our history, it is very particularly a leadership of discontinuity. By that,

I mean that much of what we have known and loved is ending and the new appears very uncertain. In this way, we are totally part of the people of today who daily face uncertainty about their jobs and relationships, about their economic stability, their safety in the face of war, terrorism, and their concern about the effects of climate change.

Faith-filled leadership is then the leadership we exercise when God intervenes in a surprising way in the life of our congregations both within the congregation and also in the contexts in which our members are living and working. It is the leadership we exercise as a way of life, a way of discernment when the known becomes the unknown and when the sacred history we know becomes the mystery we don't know.

When the trodden path fades out or becomes unfamiliar or different, we find ourselves at a crossroads. This is true of leaders and all leadership being exercised by members in their ministries within our congregations. Leadership exercised at a time when the horizon of our planning and strategy is shifting much closer to the everyday action and planning for an unknown future is unpredictable. Plans made at one large system event or general chapter can seem outdated and almost irrelevant sometimes when the next chapter comes round. The pace of change is speeding up because the events of the world are driving it—this world in which God is already present and at work.

This has implications for the way we exercise faith. I deliberately use the words *exercise faith* because this is what we are called to do by a path of prayer, dialogue, discernment, and ministry at this time of unknowing. Discernment is a way of life, not something we do only when we have a decision to make. Leaders are called today to be 'full of faith', filled with faith *not by will but by gift*.

The Gold of Transforming Roles

To recognize and claim this gift of God to each one of us, leaders and members, is an essential basis for development. We claim the gift by praying for it, by putting it into action—not just by saying we have it!

What can be more prophetic than collaborating in the incarnation of the word of God in our times? The people we engage with in our contexts—social, political, cultural, economic—are waiting for this word and perplexed by our lives when we don't have the courage or language to speak a word of faith that comes out of the depths of our hearts and our lived contemplation. I was once in a global organizational conference in Oman, and some of the participants were also from Saudi Arabia and other countries in the Middle East. Once they got to know my colleague and myself, the big question they had was this: 'Why do we not know about you people?'

We do, however, sometimes have a problem of integrating with and engaging corporately with the societies or contexts in which we operate because often the language we use is understood by very few people and not by those engaged in civic, economic, and political life; it comes across as piety or moralistic language, and we need to seek a new language that enables people to find meaning. Despite my interest in the actual words we use, there is another dimension that we can attend to, and that is the language that is given to us by the Spirit of God at the appropriate moment. This language seeps out through our very pores because of the passion, the fire, and the love we have in our hearts and gives life and meaning to the people we engage with and also to our own members and those with whom we work.

Perhaps we don't understand it, but certainly, the signs are that life is changing dramatically and God is asking something

Discerning the Gold in Human Experience

new of congregations. People say it is a crisis of numbers, but is it not rather a crisis of faith, our inability to recognize God with us, and discern these new and challenging signs, that strip us of power, control, clarity, and certainty and leave us dependent on the living God to map out our way? We need all our engagement, our faith, and our trust to listen and wait patiently for this new word God is speaking in our times. We also need each other's hope and courage to strengthen our faith.

However, I am struck so often by the lamentation I hear in organizations and communities, the constant complaint about overwork, loss of meaning, and even despair. What has happened to our joy? To our sense of purpose? Are we failing to see the signs of the times and putting our energy into yesterday's solutions instead of developing and engaging with the new reality so evident around us? Covid-19 has stopped the world in its tracks and every organization with it. Tragic situations have emerged related to death, sickness, economy, and mental health, and many organizations have come to a halt while others are engaging online in a creative way.

As we explore this new reality, perfect structures and plans are not the answer. They are only a tool to carry the charism into the context. Sometimes despite all the work, the meetings, the external changes, the heart of the congregation remains dry and unfed because leaders and members have lost their *sense of purpose.*

I am drawing attention to faith as the essence of our lives before plunging into some of the challenging and internal matters facing leaders and members—leaders and members because unless members authorize their leaders to lead, there is no leadership. One of the signs of a dysfunctional organization is a lack of clear authority, and sadly, this is true in many congregations today when the leaders are not free or authorized to lead because there is a misconception of what it means for members to participate. Both leaders and members get confused about the distinction between participating through consultation and discernment in decision making and where the authority lies to make the decision. This means, in some cases, that critical decisions are never made because consensus cannot be reached.

There is another aspect to clear authority *and that is in relation to the action taken in role to serve the mission and purpose of the congregation.* We need to recognize that in any organization, of which a congregation is one, there are different and complementary roles, and we can authorize each other to fulfil the ministry attached to the role on behalf of the whole congregation. This is a source of great freedom and energy for the sake of the mission. Each one exercises authority in their own role.

The context of the world economic crisis is pointing out to us that the meaning of leadership has become somewhat ambiguous. Corruption and betrayal in the economic and business sector has made us all examine our own corruption and collusions with these systems. The authority in these operations has been exposed, and many are disillusioned and angry about the flaws that have been discovered. No one quite knows who to blame. Especially at a time where organizational structures tend to be more horizontal rather than hierarchical, it becomes more and more demanding to deal with the complexities of interdependent relationships—by that, I mean how each part of the organization relates to the other part and to the whole. Autonomy or independence of one part of an organization to the whole is an outworn concept in a world of networks and globalization.

Discerning the Gold in Human Experience

A relationship of trust and mutuality is called for between each of the parts and building this is the task of leaders and members. It seems important to diffuse the projections that members are participants in the leaders' authority rather than having their own inner authority in relation to the commitment they have made to live the life through their task or ministry to which, of course, they are sent by the congregation and to which they are accountable.

At the same time as there is a crisis of leadership, members continue through their ministries, often in very hidden ways, to bring about significant change even while feeling their contributions are just a drop in the ocean and at times detached from where the leaders themselves are at in their reflection.

Gathering the wisdom of what is happening in the context of the ministries exercised by the members and leaders corporately is part of the way to having the reflected on and prayed over material for the ongoing discernment about the way God is leading us forward. We can learn much today from our new understanding of the evolutionary nature of our Cosmos. Everything is only a step towards the overall fullness of being. Decisions are a part of that evolutionary process, not a defining new reality. This can be an empowering and freeing experience for those in leadership who find decision making hard. No decision is forever.

As with the cosmos, the task of expanding our awareness always requires effort and patience and what we are considering here is what needs to be done in our organizations, so we do not merely survive but evolve and transform—not in terms of numbers or structures but in purpose. How is our congregation engaging itself through its dynamics with the people in a particular context so as to carry out its mission and to expand that mission in new and creative ways so we too are part of a new creation? And how are we training people so that our work continues once we leave the area? This is very different from just being busy or suffering from fatigue because we are overstretched. Just as the cosmos is interconnected, so too are leaders, members, the organization, the context interconnected and constantly informing each other so everyone is engaged in new learning and insights. In fact, this is what we do through dialogue, sharing, and interconnection with each other. The challenge is to experience this in the new cosmic reality of which we are only an infinitesimal part.

Leading and managing organizations requires boundaries—obviously the boundary of the mission in the sense that it is the mission that unifies, motivates, and clarifies who we are for ourselves and for others as we understand it. It is through the corporate mission that we relate to and seek to make a difference in the context, but it is much more than that. Boundaries outline what is considered to be inside the organization and what is to stay outside. If understood well, they are not functioning as barriers. They can also be thought of as interfaces: places and moments of contact between different parts and processes of a complex social system called organization. The way these parts interconnect and harness the energy is of great significance to the relatedness of each part and indeed of each one to the whole. The inclusion of each one concerns the mission and the way it is fulfilled, according to the founding spirit and purpose of the organization and the needs of the people in context. The illusion among leaders and members is to believe it all depends on the leadership. The move from dependence to self-authorizing and interdependence changes the very face of congregations and organizations today. This is difficult because the members and leaders can be on different parts of the spectrum and deeply influenced by their local culture.

The dynamic nature of every organization comes about in practice not only with an aware leadership but by the engagement of the members with each other and their ministry within the purpose. At the very core of the organization—*uncontrolled by anyone*—there is an interactive process that produces more than just the interactions: it creates a social system with a culture of its own, and despite our best processes of asking members to engage with a particular specific ministry, roles are *also* attributed to them in the context and taken up by the people within it. The nature of role often depends on the capabilities of people to accept or reject what others attribute to them besides what leadership attributes to them. This happens to everyone from a very early age, and transformation of these roles in systems requires direct access into the process of transforming the system as a whole. The constant dialogue then among members, including leaders, is part of the growing self-awareness and evolution. Where relationship between leaders and members is hostile or threatening to this evolution, it is the planet itself that is being damaged, as we are part of one story of humanity.

The changing nature of authority

This is where I come to the nature of authority in congregations today. Because members are more aware of themselves in role, because the context is more complex and demanding, and because consecrated life is seeking meaning in cultures and society, there is a definite move among members to be more involved in their own process and hence in the process of decision-making in the congregations. It is not enough anymore, though fundamental, to make clear distinctions between the role of leaders and members, because the social systems are so interdependent that a new way needs to evolve, be understood, and be lived out. Communication and dialogue are of the essence of good discernment.

Even as the significance of formal rank and job descriptions seems to be in decline, how a person engages in role with the purpose of the mission through their ministry is vital for vibrant and faith-filled leadership and membership.

Embodying a role may be seen to give life to something that belongs to the congregation as a whole. Therefore, how we conduct ourselves in role reflects, to a certain degree, the authority invested in each one to act on behalf of the others in the whole congregation. The underlying issue for the individuals involved is what this means for accountability. A member cannot take up a role or be accountable unless there is a clear mandate, a clear aim for their role in relation to the mission, and a system of evaluation and accountability built into the sending on a mission on behalf of the whole.

Relationship and Relatedness

Much of what I am saying above is about relatedness to the mission of the organization. However especially in community life human relationships and personalities are also important. When relationships are whole and healthy then the leader and members can exercise their ministry with joy and peace. Sadly, in every organization we meet dysfunction – all of us carry it to a certain extent - but when dysfunction starts to take the upper hand it seeps the energy from leaders and members. Today there are very significant helps for human growth and many congregations avail of these.

So-Wha Kwak snd translating for Christine Anderson in Korea

CHAPTER 7

The Gold of Crisis and Faith

Faith and Culture

Many programs in different settings are focusing currently on the understanding of culture and intercultural processes. In Faith and Praxis for Global Leadership, the focus is consistent in working at the integration of faith and culture. The number and variety of cultures we work with help us to stand in awe at the richness of the world and the mystery of our place within it. Each human person has a way of giving expression to a particular and transcendent dimension of human life. No one of us is an expert on culture in our organizations, but what we can explore is the dimension of faith in culture. A faith that does not heed the culture in which it is embedded is never fully accepted, thought out, or deeply lived. We think of the clashes that break out in various countries at a time of elections or particular national problems, and we see how quickly faith can dissolve and be replaced by violence and sometimes extreme cruelty. Culture, however, is the whole of human activity, intelligence, and emotions. It embraces the human quest for finding meaning within our human customs and ethics. The original encounter of faith and culture demands a point of discontinuity from the known way. We see the example of God inviting Abraham to 'leave your own country, your kindred and your father's house' (Genesis 12:1) and 'by faith he sojourned in the land of promise living in tents'. This cultural break was the point at which Abraham's call to follow God began, and it is an example of what happens in the human heart when God surprises us and intervenes in our lives. This cultural break cannot just simply widen our knowledge about culture but challenges us to a commitment of our being in relation to our values and beliefs. The encounter of faith with different cultures creates something new, and the split we often meet between faith, values, and beliefs with culture is the drama of our days as we embrace a global world with multicultural populations in many countries.

Today, throughout the world, many people are isolated and marginalized in society because of the economic and political situation. They can feel powerless and isolated because of their culture. At the same time, there is a new culture developing, a global cultural revolution as we discover new ways of communicating and new techniques. This is bringing about a cultural revolution that is developing a fundamental reshaping of the elements by which we understand our world within the whole universe. A new age in human history is emerging in the global world. There is an urgency to enable each one to express the principles and values which make up the ethos of a people. It isn't enough to focus on dress or food or even imports and exports. We know in our time how faith has been at times like an over garment in the lives of people e.g., at the time of the elections, when faith can be cast aside in favour of tribal loyalties in various countries where genocide has been practiced in the name of culture. We just need to scratch the surface of our own experience so we can each realize personally how deeply our own racism and prejudices run in our bloodstream. After the war in the Balkans, I was part of a team in a peacebuilding program. I remember one day sitting with a Croatian and a Serb. The Serb put her arm around the Croatian and said she knew her people had been at war with their people but, in fact, she had never met a Croat! Some of her prejudices and ignorance were being challenged by this very human dimension. The human story can sometimes, but not always, overcome the prejudices.

Another example happened when I was working in Asia with two peoples who were also just coming out of war. In this particular peacebuilding exercise, I asked the participants to meet in national groups to work on the rituals, myths, and stories in their tradition and come back to present the result of their work to each other. There was amazing synchronicity in their discoveries, and this led to a willingness to explore what it would feel like to work together. We cannot underestimate the pain and courage of that when family members on both sides had recently been killed.

That is why it is so important to understand discernment. It is not just a question of a religious feeling but also a sifting of the heart that leads to a demanding personal and corporate commitment to the deepest values we seek to express in our faith. In doing so, and in seeking inner freedom, we face our prejudices and obstacles to true peace and encourage and work in a nonviolent way.

Crisis and Faith in organizational practice

Organizations and groups are like people. They move in and out of crisis situations as they grow and develop. The work we do in the analysis of role sessions is based on critical incidents being experienced by the leader or the team at a particular time. Some of the issues that are brought to us have to do with cultural differences, personality difficulties, and disagreement about whether structures fit the purpose of the mission today. Some leaders in role analysis focus on authority and power and worry about diminishment and expansion of the organization or financial problems, especially concerning the sustainability of the organization. These are just a few examples, and they are the elements of working together to enable the person or group to find the resources within themselves and their own system to move forward in the development of the mission. Many of them focus on cultural differences and the struggle to work positively with them.

In our work as consultants to these leaders, crisis is not only endurable but necessary for the very life of the organization. An organization without crisis is a very boring organization indeed! What stimulates and enlivens it is not the crisis itself but the way the crisis is engaged with. Crisis calls us not just to solve issues but to a conversion of heart, to an inner freedom to have the courage to discern a different way forward. The human experience is sacred in its essence, and it is the human experience of success and failure which is the very ground for the healthy development of the mission.

What happens to our faith when a crisis hits? Often, we look around for someone to blame, for circumstances to change, for our ideal scenario. No amount of blaming, no number of changed circumstances, no ideal scenario can replace the in-depth search for meaning behind the events. In times of crisis, we find that we exercise faith differently, knowing that our all-loving God can use even this crisis for the good of the situation. At times, it is hard to see this, especially when despondency seems to have the upper hand. However, our faith, deeply lived, is transformative, and in the midst of darkness, we can also experience joy and new hope.

Despite all our good efforts in the organizations that we lead and manage, we can feel disorientated by the crisis, feeling as though God has deserted us. Crisis often happens when we are very busy and believe we don't have the time to enter into deeper reflection. This is often one of the discoveries in the organizational role analysis session. In it, the leader has withdrawn from the day-to-day running of the organization to reflect on the conscious and unconscious dynamics at play in particular circumstances. It is amazing the contribution that time and space can offer to an overwrought leader, who can be disorientated by so many elements coming at her or him from so many circumstances. What happens in the session is that they take time to recognize the crisis. Too much busyness in the organization prevents this quiet and detailed reflection. A crisis can work towards growth and depth in the organization or towards disintegration. Most lives are too busy in organizations today, but one of the aspects of our work that is fundamental for a healthy organization is the ability to take time to reflect. Reflection is work!

A crisis indeed needs to be managed. When the leader or member discovers there is a crisis, there are at least two possible ways of dealing with it: to hold on courageously and with flexibility to the core values which give strength when things are going well, or to throw one's hands up in dismay and despair and allow our ways of thinking to become angry, bitter, resentful, and self-pitying. A crisis can be looked on as a grace, and awareness of the power of the good and evil spirit in the life of the organization is essential. If it is not there, the crisis can tear the heart out of an organization and especially from the leader and the members involved-

St Ignatius was a great believer in taking time to contemplate the events of the day to derive the greatest learning from them. This is so true in relation to the organizations we lead and manage. It isn't enough to recover from the crisis but indeed to understand it, tracing the ways the crisis nearly led us away from our original purpose. A crisis can bring out the very best or the very worst in us! This depends on how we relate to the core values. The most serious crisis leading to serious conflict comes about when there is a disagreement about the core values at the very heart of the mission. This cannot be covered over but needs to be brought to light in a spirit of transparency. At that point, some members walk away and change jobs or leave the organization if they are not able to dialogue openly about their differences.

Crisis in an organization not only disorientates, but it can also be very confusing. The temptation is for the sake of peace to settle for the familiar and prevent ourselves from experiencing the new space, the go-between space where we work together to make sense of the whole crisis and hope the experience has been a healthy process for renewal and not rigidity. Organizations need to change dramatically in our days, and that is why the sifting of the experience in faith in a spirit of discernment is so fundamental to the well-being of the whole. Discernment is a way of life and not an organizational tool. This means that to discern and deal with critical situations, Christian leaders today are invited to enter deeply into the Paschal Mystery of Life, Death, and Resurrection. In doing so, they expand their horizons and give depth to their living, entering more fully into the mystery of God with us, in us, and working through us. This is the gift and grace of crisis, and explore this source of new life and transformation for the organization.

CHAPTER 8

The Gold of Clarity and Confusion

Experience is gold, but some experiences do not always feel like it. Clarity is brought about in organizations in many different ways. As has been said, clarity about how to engage with the system in which we are working means grasping the boundaries of the organizations.

A boundary is like our skin. It is flexible and serves us so well. However, if the skin is not there or is broken, the body becomes infected and bleeds. This happens to organizations too. If the boundaries are not clear and flexible, the organization loses its unique identity and is just like many others. An example of this would be of NGOs working on projects in the same area. Each organization has its own boundary, but these boundaries are damaged when comparisons are made, in relation, for example, to type of work, time off and working conditions, staff ratios, and financing. I see this happening in voluntary organizations and faith-based organizations working in projects for a long time. The boundaries can become blurred, and staff can become dissatisfied and disillusioned, especially if they lose touch with the vision and purpose of their own organization. This vision and purpose encapsulate the values, beliefs, and ethos of their organization. The skin or boundary holds all the activities of the organization together and is, in effect, what enables us to be clear about the mission.

I saw this clearly in Liberia after the war. The country was flooded, with NGOs all trying to help in a desperate situation. For some of these NGOs, they were very well-financed, and the salaries were good. For others, particularly faith-based voluntary organizations, they were like the poor relations! They were idealistic, wedded to particular values until the going was tough and they realized they didn't have the financial resources to fly out for a break or go to particular hotels or clubs to relax and socialise. For the most part, they understood this, and although they felt the difference, they accepted it. Some, however, could not cope with the loneliness, the boredom in the evenings, and the exhaustion from the work and could become dissatisfied and start to make comparisons.

Boundaries and barriers are different. A *barrier* is a block or impediment to free movement. An example would be when an organization gets cut off from its context and is no longer making the impact it was founded to make. It becomes a closed system.

No organization is totally clear on its *boundaries* all the time. Having a keen and overtly expressed sense of purpose helps clarity, but it is not the whole story. Organizations are made up of human beings who are going through their own inner processes and outer realities. There is always movement going on, and there has to be in a really healthy and well-functioning individual and organization. However, we deal with these movements differently. Take the example of a member who suddenly finds herself in a personal crisis. Some members despite their own inner suffering or family worries are able to go on working to task and don't let the organization suffer because of their circumstances. Others fall apart and their work consequently falls apart. Part of the difficulty is that organizations have problems dealing with vulnerability, and this can be taken to extremes.

Vulnerability as a resource

Once I was working with a group of organizational consultants in a country in the Southern Hemisphere. The purpose of their organization was to assist the local government to turn around a situation of serious fraud. My work with them lasted a week, and during that week, we had two sessions for each one of them to have a role consultation. By midweek, the group seemed to be stuck, and I myself was feeling stuck! Then, one of these men came forward for his second session. He had been among the apparently more cheerful persons in the group. As he entered the room for the consultation—in front of his colleagues—he gave me a very cheery greeting. The session started in silence, and I waited to see what he was going to present that morning. After a few moments, the tears started running down his face. It took him time to blurt out the issue. In fact, he had recently discovered that he had a life threatening illness. He had taken a week off from work, and his wife had phoned the office to say they were going away on holiday. And there he was, back at work, and he hadn't found the way to tell his colleagues. His worry was that if they knew, he wouldn't get the contracts, and he needed the money. My question that morning resonated not just with the participant in front of me but with the whole group: Where is the

The Gold of Clarity and Confusion

place for vulnerability in this organization? This question opened out a whole new dynamic for the rest of the week. I heard in later months that not only had the permission to name their own vulnerabilities enabled the consultants themselves to work more openly and justly as a team but that it had enabled them to open out the question of vulnerability with their clients.

The importance of connections and communication

People can become detached from the organization, not deliberately but by circumstances. Take the example of a missionary working hundreds of miles away in the bush or in the desert. Communications are bad, and the villages are in such need of support. It can be years before they hear or see another member of the congregation, and they can lose their sense of belonging. They are trusted to go on living out the purpose of the organization, but many factors intervene. Sometimes, the congregation has grown so big and expanded all over the world. This presents a problem for the international leadership to visit every part of it. I came across one group of women who had not had a visit from their international leadership in twelve years because of the political situation! Without this ongoing connection, they had become totally absorbed by local issues and no longer saw any point of belonging to the international organization.

I remember a doctor in Lithuania who had trained as a priest in the underground. After independence, he was asked to be the nominal head of the school in transition until the incoming head had had time for in service training. I literally saw a little boy run up to him in the middle of a service to tell him he was sick and the priest turning to take his pulse. There he was in three roles—priest, doctor, teacher—one assigned to him by his religious congregation—the teacher, one accepted by vocation, the priest, and one inbuilt in him as a doctor! We all carry many different roles; the important thing is to be clear in which one we are working. However, in many cases, it isn't clear. We get confused and can feel more a part of the people we are serving than the organization we originally joined! We knowingly accept that some mistakes are inevitable, and that is where vulnerability and the ability for compassion and reconciliation are so important.

One of the main sources of confusion lies in personality and cultural clashes. Does the fact that someone disagrees with my opinion mean that they reject me or me them? There is a lot of tension, conflict, and lack of understanding buried in this concept. The ideas of a person are only an expression; they are not the fullness of that person. In role consultations, so often, the question of personality clashes comes up and the inability we all struggle with in working with projections. If we take them all seriously, we will betray the end for which our organizations are created. If we don't learn something from them, we become stuck in a mire of confusion and narcissism. This applies not only to individuals but also, at times, to nations. Sometimes, when a new leader is named, we hear comments like, 'Not another European or Japanese or African or American.' Often, the persons making the comments have never met someone from that country and only have information from the media or from gossip. In other words, it can be destructive and sow violence or disquiet. This is not an invitation to say nothing, but as St Paul says, 'to speak the truth in love' (Ephesians 4:15). Truth can cost, and it is healthy when the atmosphere in the organization is open to hear. If the members are not free to speak their truth, then a spirit of defensiveness builds up and marginalizes the person. This sort of dialogue, or lack of it, takes place particularly when it is a question of change. Patrick Keegan in the Christian Worker Movement used to encourage us not to worry about change because change is brought about in surprising ways. This example sticks in my mind. Working in Sri Lanka before and after the tsunami were two very different experiences. Before the tsunami, I worked with Jesuit Refugee Service on the coast with various projects. We were on the move a lot and slept where we could. One night, some of us were sleeping on mats on the floor inside the hut, and others decided to sleep under the stars. It was a beautiful clear night to start with, but in the early morning, torrential rain came, and those outside rushed inside. Those inside moved along to make room, except for one person. She lay totally still and apparently asleep. We stepped over her at great inconvenience. The next morning, I asked her if she hadn't heard us.

'Yes,' she replied, 'but, you see, it was my *great silence*, and we don't speak or interact with others from nine o'clock at night until eight in the morning!' This was a rule of her congregation.

Well, a few months later, the tsunami had come and we as a team were back in Sri Lanka, collaborating with the displaced as they tried to pick up the pieces of their lives. Out of the crowd, a woman approached me and asked me if I recognized her. I had to admit that I didn't, and she told me she was the one 'with the great silence'. All that strict and structured lifestyle had been washed away by a critical event of nature, and now that their institutions had been destroyed, she with her community were out among the people living the same mission but in a much less structured way. A combination of crisis and nature had brought about change!

Sometimes we experience tsunamis in our own lives—different in nature but substantial enough to bring about change for good and bad. Covid-19 certainly brought the world to a stop, and everyone made so many changes because of the pandemic. Besides the devastating effect on the economy and on some domestic situations, we are witnessing a change of attitude, a burgeoning of kindness and compassion for each other as well as a deep concern about mental illness and loneliness in our societies. The stress on uniformity can be replaced by creativity and adaptability. Instead of individualism, corporate concern is nurtured, and a spirit of inclusion enables a sense of belonging no matter how dispersed the members are.

The question remains as to whether we want to go back to the normal we knew or to create a new more ecological and just way of being.

Social Justice and Spirituality

The discovery of God's mercy and loving presence amid the vulnerability enables individuals and groups to realize that God works here preferentially and that this very place is the springboard for real change and development. We witnessed this in the examples already given. This discovery is the most powerful tool and one which is most effective. A good social, political, cultural, and economic analysis can bring the group to a crisis point about its identity in the local and international context. This leads to issues of conflict, negotiation, repentance, reconciliation, and the realigning of the reality as it is experienced currently with the desired vision. There is no inappropriate place to start working with groups and organizations in their quest for social justice. Social justice is at the heart of the work of Faith and Praxis. God is always waiting to enter into a deeper relationship with us, and God is also present, eager, and loving as the organization struggles in its evolution to take its place in society. God is already present and active in the affairs of the world and we seek as citizens in society to rediscover Him in the social, economic, political, and cultural realities in which we are engaged.

The staff member who enters into this dynamic must at least be willing to acknowledge that effort intuition and grace are at work and that God is present in the chaos. 'For I know the plans I have for you, says the Lord, plans for welfare and not for disaster, to give you a future and a hope' (Jeremiah 29:11).

One of the big assumptions in the spiritual exercises of St Ignatius is that there is no disparity between what is best for the person and what God wants for us. Today, it is easy to become lost in the complexity of the struggle to integrate life and faith. We struggle with language, muse over the gap between what is heard in the Word and what values and beliefs motivate business and industry, and yet, St Ignatius encourages us not to run away from reality but to encounter it at its most profound point. The challenge is to face up to the real ultimate that life is all about and to explore through our experience what it means to be fully alive.

This requires a basic desire to live in faith and to acknowledge God present in the whole of our reality. It also requires that we acknowledge that the effort of organizations working on the edge of change is enhanced and threaded through with intuition and grace. Faith is a fundamental disposition for this kind of searching—the type of faith which does not necessarily know the answers but which is willing to acknowledge that God's action in the life of the members is greater than they could ever ask or desire. So, this dynamic requires a coming before God with open hands, ready and willing to receive any gifts that may be given. We cannot program God's generosity. Jesus accepted the violent, the passionate, lustful, and avaricious but frequently rebuked his followers for their lack of faith.

And so one of the texts for staff and professional associates as they enter into a change process is: Now to the One who by the power at work within us is able to do far more abundantly than all that we ask or imagine (Ephesians 3:20).

The exercises offered to us by Saint Ignatius are indeed what they say they are—exercises, detailed exercises of examining one's life from many different perspectives. However, in my own experience, I have noted many of the experiences of the spiritual exercises are also common to organizations. The dynamic of the paschal mystery is always to be found in the group with which one is working, because this is human experience, and this spirituality offers us one way of working with it. It is an affective experience, and in today's language, we would talk about taking into account the conscious and the unconscious processes. There is a thoroughness and depth about the way a group or organization can be worked with—not linearly but in a spiral dynamic. This thoroughness is grasped by the staff member to the extent that the person is engaged at depth with effort, intuition and grace, and can enable the members of the training group or organization to be collaborating with God in bringing about change in their context. However, he also needs to recognize that it does not all depend on efficiency and good planning, as there are many 'unknowns' in the life of faith and the unconscious behaviour of the group.

And so, the perspective by which we entered into our work is one which acknowledges God's love underpinning the groups in all their dimensions—personnel, resources, leadership, participation, and management. In the early stages of the programs, the members are brought back to their root values and given the opportunity to review their own story. From where do the participants originate in terms of values and beliefs? This is appropriate for any group, no matter what its faith base, as long as the person is willing to struggle with and identify the dynamic of effort, intuition, and grace within themselves and the group as they work. What is the mission of the group in its overall organization in society? How can participants be helped to identify their role in this society? Is there the will within the work for its members to take on the corporate desire or mission of Christ?

The principle and foundation of God's love is not to be separated from the discovery of God in all aspects of creation. For the participants, a question to be explored is this: what does it mean for participants to share in a more just and healthy society in which each person has a unique contribution to make? How do they keep themselves in right relationships with the environment and with the whole of creation? This brings to the fore issues about the dignity of the person, ecology and the distribution of resources, particularly in the world context. For programs and organizations, as well as for individuals, this can be a desert experience where reality is faced in all its starkness and needs to seek ways of being transformed in context.

There is, however, a change dynamic which is fundamental in this process. It is the simple belief that everything does not depend on us, and that events in the universe also impact and enrich our growth.

The effects of globalization and internationality are seen most dramatically in the increasing gap between the rich and the poor, with the effects of starvation, death, civil war, and displacement of peoples. Any faith-related organization which seriously reflects must accept that it is part of this wider sinful situation in which the distribution of wealth is in the hands of the privileged few. From looking at the international context, the focus shifts to the local scene and the implications for the immediate context. Whether participants become aware of it or not, what they are really struggling with is issues of authority, power, and control in the context of the gods or images of God which are carried in their minds. For Christians, this is crucial to develop a theological basis of God's loving mercy rather than harsh judgement and rejection. It is in the context of social sin that the group can come face to face with the wonder of being corporately alive—that moment of wonder when it is poised between despair and self-recrimination and the will to live. For Ignatius, to be alive is to be the recipient of gifts and favours. This is the experience he wants to share with us—an experience of wonder at the goodness of God towards him. This gratitude awakens a desire for contemplation and a recognition of forces at work which are not only bigger than ourselves but powerfully at work in our organizations too. A sick society is like an infection, and often, sickness in family, work, community, and organizations is rife because we don't know how to deal with greed, avarice, pride, ambition, and competition. Ways need to be found to reveal this gently to ourselves and our groups, in a way which is real and not judgmental. Expressing our vulnerability is only one route.

The greatest crisis facing all of us today – whether rich or poor, no matter which culture or nationality, is that of climate change. The research of the scientists is telling us of the dire state our ecological system is in and of how little time we have to make serious life style and industrial changes to meet it.

CHAPTER 9

The Gold of Wisdom in Experience

The cost of taking up our role as citizens in society

It is not enough for individuals to profess to act justly, but how does this justice permeate our lands, our environment, our work practices, families, and neighbourhood communities? This is one of the biggest challenges that each person struggles with: What difference will my little contribution make to some of the major threats to our world system? I remember a woman in one of my groups who came into the program with no sense of her own self-esteem and dignity. The groups she worked in during the following year transformed her confidence, and after that year, she had found her voice and was articulate for basic human rights in a residents' association in a very poor part of the city. This demonstrates that for her resources and strength are found in the group and are not dependent only on the staff team or presenters.

For participants to engage with society in its context, they are given the opportunity to enter into a process in relation to the difference they want to make in their context. Depending on the outcome of these reflections will be the way in which the participants position themselves in society. It is not a simple thing to do, and there is a cost to it, certainly for the staff group and for participants who choose to follow through on their new learning. There is a cost of both energy and emotions as people can become worn out not just by the demands of making a choice but by the psychological and emotional challenges this proposes to them. Sometimes, the lack of resources of finance can impede the desired action, and this can lead to disillusionment and frustration. Another source of energy loss is that often many people don't feel they have sufficient education or charisma to work in groups or to make changes and need the support of each other.

In our experience, there are *critical choices* to be made as to where one desires to situate oneself in society—for example, with the poor and downtrodden or working with people trapped in addictions or violent relationships, and often with those who have lost a sense of meaning and are facing despair. What choices do we have to make so that people can earn their living with dignity and at the same time the organizations they work in can be respected, effective, and financially viable? These are among the issues struggled with in the groups, but the fundamental choice is in the desire of each one to bring about change in society. The social pastoral process was a great help here—articulating and naming the experience and analysing it in the light of the economic, political, cultural and social realities. This analysis takes time and effort. Following that, we share the texts of scripture or inspirational texts of our tradition that will enable us to make the necessary changes and then commit to some small or big change of attitudes or situations. There was a man in one of the groups who was working in an arms factory. Years later, I met him again, and he told me that because of the social analysis he had done in the program, he had decided to give up his job because it was preparing arms for war and death. Now he was earning much less, but with his family, he had opened a small hotel and enjoyed giving life and resourcing people who came for a rest.

Suffering, Death, and Grieving in Society

Many aspects of society or church are dying or already dead, and this causes intense suffering to the members. The importance of facing death in order to free the organization to grieve and to transcend death leads to new life and creativity. What change processes are in place and what is the strategy for the life and sustainability of the work? How is grief faced and worked with within the organization? How do we corporately exercise faith in life in moments of crisis and turmoil? In brokenness and fragmentation in the organization, how is faith a resource for wholeness? What moves the members of the organization to greater faith, hope, and love, and what leads them to disillusionment and despair? The movements of consolation and desolation of an organization are as it were the barometers of its spiritual and psychological health and wholeness. Some members in Craighead Institute had the opportunity to work at these issues in small guided groups and also in individual sessions. Having worked in many countries, we discovered that the human dynamic is always very similar despite the huge disparity in finances, cultures, and educational backgrounds.

We cannot ignore the importance of prayer in organizational change. It is especially in prayer that we find the inner freedom to make the changes necessary and to engage with the living God who is already at work in society.

Growth and Diminishment

Through our work, we have the opportunity to work with organizations that are expanding or dying. In some cases, they are dying in Europe but coming to new life in Africa, Asia, and Oceania. In this case, a lot of resituating of resources of finance and personnel is going on, including structures for healthy leadership and membership.

However, I think of two organizations that are currently dying. The first made the decision clearly and worked over five years to ensure the wellbeing of the leaders and members. They are no longer developing in the countries of Europe and in Africa. They have finished training people in Africa to take over their work in schools and hospitals and feel good about that. This group is living with the satisfaction of a mission carried out and fulfilled. The work with them included work on their finances, the handing over of their company and trust, the downsizing of buildings and projects, and the withdrawal from countries where the members had invested their lives. So much pain and grief! Through the time of transition, each one had the opportunity to process their deep emotions, doubts, fears, and anguish. It was demanding for them, and they mostly faced it with courage and acceptance. Some did not, and that made it difficult for the leadership. Together, we worked on each aspect of the dynamic until those who were doubting were able to negotiate a way forward for themselves and the leadership team were willing to compromise. No solution is ever perfect because we are human beings and owed the respect and dignity necessary to function well.

The second organization was very different. The evidence was that they were dying with just a handful of members left. However,

Discerning the Gold in Human Experience

they wanted to regenerate and bring in new members to run an outdated system. Although they accepted that it was outdated, they refused to take steps to move on. They were supported in this by a board who had convinced them that they could continue and had their eye on the extensive resources of land and buildings. This was more difficult to work with because the critical choice had not been made. In the end, after much heart-searching, they decided to do nothing and just let the organization find its own way forward. Sometimes this works, but most often, it doesn't. Then it leads not to crisis but to emergency management!

A consultant is not there to save the organization but to facilitate their process at a particular moment in time. Some decisions today in congregations require radical decisions, but leadership is often trapped by the intransigence of some members who don't want to leave the lands and people in which they have invested their lives. This is so understandable and yet difficult to steer forward.

In organizations today, because of the diminishment in some parts of the world and the expansion in others, many organizations ask facilitators or consultants to work with them on their structures. This means working with both leaders and members on their understanding of their mission as it is being renewed in the context of today, exploring the resources of personnel and financial viability and sustainability of each part of the whole.

Sustainability of the works is a big issue, particularly in the developing world. As resources decrease in the north, leaders and members must be fully involved in designing the new scheme of things—in other words, taking care of their own sustainability and the new potential structures. Imaginative and creative ways are being found to ensure that the work done through development education is not lost. This is why Faith and Praxis made Training of Trainers a priority and sought to enable local people to do what we as a staff group are doing. In some cases, this was very successful, and in others, it remains fragile.

Mr. Jules Adanbéché from Benin, working in a training group in Rwanda

CHAPTER 10

The Gold of Collective Wisdom

The Infinite Dynamic of Co-Creation

The Covid-19 pandemic is a powerful example of how the world is developing a new paradigm without all the strategies and academic theses of human beings. We are caught up in a new reality which is wreaking destruction in some systems—health, education, economy, and business to give a few examples. At the same time, it is bringing to birth new ways of relating and communicating, expressions of compassion and service, and of course a multitude of questions as to why this is happening at all. No one has the answers, except perhaps the scientists, who are working to create the new vaccines that we hope will save us. The greatest crisis facing the world however is not the pandemic but climate change!

Within this dynamic of reflective experience, those who thrive and enjoy the journey are often those individuals and organizations who are not afraid of their own questions. So many opportunities are open to us to deepen the meaning of our reflection. For some, this comes through communal prayer, faith sharing and spiritual accompaniment, sharing the journey with other companions. For others, they are enabled to grow and develop through counselling and growth therapy. In organizations, it can be external consultation of a team together or individual supervision on a regular basis. It does not matter how we grow as long as we have the courage and confidence to leave the old behind and move forward in the light of new discoveries.

My passion is and has been throughout my life the integration of life and faith. At one stage, I thought they would one day become one, but now, I know that they will always be held in healthy tension. It is this tension and the inward search that keeps us exploring. Throughout this journey, I have learned new things. When I was in school, we were often asked what we thought about something. This was good but was based on the filters that we ourselves exercised in our mentality. Now I know that that is not enough—based on our knowledge and research which are important, we are called to be the great explorers of our times, to be the co-creators of a new world at a time of unprecedented challenge.

During the pandemic of Covid-19, on 27 March 2020, Pope Francis stood on the steps of St Peter's Basilica, alone and in the pouring rain, to bless the world at this critical time. He referred to the story of Jesus calming the storm as in the Gospel of St Mark (4:35–41).

He said:

Like the disciples in the Gospel we were caught off-guard by an unexpected, turbulent storm. We have realised that we are on the same boat, all of us fragile and disorientated, but at the same time important and needed, all of us called to row together, each of us in need of comforting the other.

Sister Christine meets Pope Francis 2019

Some of the questions I have raised will be washed away and become irrelevant, but they are questions that have come out of experience – an experience lived in groups of people engaging and analysing the context all the time. Each of us has our own questions and has the opportunity to reflect and raise them for ourselves. Organizations are not static beings. They need to be worked at all the time. It is so true that when we think one part of an organization is well in place, we can discover that another part is in crisis. This is good because it is a living system. From quantum science, we know too that the whole is more than the sum of the parts and that no one of us can pretend to have the whole story. We are caught up in an infinite dynamic of co-creation in a universe that is evolving, and our experiences and questions are just part of that.

The nature of experience is that it is transformative. When we learn from experience, it changes the nature of our behaviour individually and corporately. However experience in itself is not enough. It needs to be analysed and reflected upon. It is our greatest skill and the one thing no one can argue with because it is the experience of our very life! To deny our experience is to deny our life.

It is our experience, couched in our own sacred history. That is why we can all experience the same event and live it differently. A new experience meets with our whole experience to create a new space.

In this book, I have endeavoured not to give answers but to share experience. In doing so, I have shared with the reader some of the questions that emerged in my life and work. My conviction is that people have the resources within themselves to forge their way forward. It is as though we are already stars in a constellation, giving light to each other on the way. How does one person's experience fit into the collective wisdom of a new paradigm? I don't know the answer to that question, but what I witness is the unrelenting search for meaning by many people and the desire to find truth in the midst of chaos.

This is where Discerning the Gold of Human Experience is only just beginning and from where the story goes on!

Faith and Praxis Associates at Gathering in Nairobi 2019

Lightning Source UK Ltd.
Milton Keynes UK
UKHW011136180521
383928UK00001B/31